WHOLE CHILD

PARENTING

AGE TWO

Concept by Claudia Sandor

WHOLE CHILD

HEALTH AND CARE
Hygiene
Diet
Routine
Yoga

COGNITIVE
DEVELOPMENT
Problem-solving
Attention
Numbers

PHYSICAL
DEVELOPMENT
Motor skills:
Sensory
Gross
Fine

SOCIAL-EMOTIONAL
DEVELOPMENT
Self-control
Friendship
Feelings

CREATIVE
DEVELOPMENT
Dramatic Play
Dance
Music
Arts

LANGUAGE
DEVELOPMENT
Communication
Speaking
Literacy

WHOLE CHILD:
AGE TWO
Six Areas of Development

WHOLE CHILD

whole \hōl\ **child** \chi-əld\ *compound noun*
1 : a child who is completely developed in all six areas

A **whole child**
grows up to reach
his or her full potential.

A **whole child** is a **well-rounded** person and lifelong learner.

A **whole child** is ready to face the world with **confidence.**

A **whole child** has **self-esteem, knowledge**, and **creativity**.

A **whole child** will live a **happy** and **fulfilling life**.

Being a successful parent starts with understanding your child.

The Whole Child Parenting Program covers every aspect of a child's cognitive, social-emotional, language, creative, physical, and health and care development.

By using clear examples, color-coded stages, simple and logical steps, age-appropriate materials and toys, developmentally appropriate activities and workbooks, and core parenting books, the Whole Child Program will change the way you think about learning.

Welcome to parenting for the new millenium!

Published by Whole Child Parenting, Inc.
Whole Child Parenting books, activity books, toys, and materials are
available at special discounts when purchased in bulk for premiums
and sales promotions as well as for fundraising or educational use.
For details, please contact us at:
sales@wholechild.co

Whole Child is a registered trademark of Whole Child, LLC
Library of Congress Control Number: 2016905515
ISBN 978-1-944930-02-8

Created by the Whole Child Education Team with:
Early Childhood Education Specialist, Erin Weekes
Book design by Willabel Tong
Art direction by Dan Marmorstein
Editorial direction by Editorial Services of Los Angeles

Visit us on the web at: www.wholechild.co
Email us at: publishing@wholechild.co

Printed in the United States of America.
1 3 5 7 9 10 8 6 4 2

Contents

What Is Whole Child Parenting?

It Is Parenting from Head to Toe

Whole child parenting involves exposing your child to everything he needs to be happy, healthy, well adjusted, smart, and developing right on track. A whole child is a well-rounded person, someone whose innate talents have been developed in every major milestone category and who is ready to face the world with confidence. A whole child has the self-esteem and knowledge to develop his true potential.

Whole child parenting is you doing what you can, with our help, to get him there. The Whole Child Parenting Program is for busy people just like you. With interactive materials that support you at every step, using toys, workbooks, activities, videos, web support, and an app, the Whole Child Parenting Program takes into account the whole child and helps you, the parent or primary caregiver, do what is necessary and best for your child at every stage, every age from infancy to five years old. It helps you parent with a purpose, giving you practical advice and materials that explain the whys and how-tos and goals of each step you take to help your child grow.

Whole child parenting is a process that begins with you. It can be overwhelming to think about the responsibility you have to your two year old in one of the most important years of his life.

Age two is a crucial year because development, in both the body and brain, is happening at a rapid pace. These first years will set the stage for how your child problem solves, communicates, socializes, and thinks for the rest of his life. That is not to say that you won't have amazing experiences with your child when he is two years old. You will have absolutely transformative experiences with your two-year-old child during these next twelve months. You will get to see life from the perspective of a person who is barely three feet tall! And **your presence and influence will always matter the most during this 24–36 months of age.** The world is constantly changing; will your child be ready for the global economy years from now? Just by reading this book you are setting yourself along the right path for being the best parent you can be for your two-year-old child.

HOW TO GET ON THE RIGHT TRACK NOW?

Whole Child Parenting: Age Two has six chapters for the six areas of development seen in the column at right. **Each area of development is assigned its own color.**

Each of the six chapters begins with a chart and summary to introduce you to the concepts and terminology in the pages ahead. Within each chapter, **you will also get real-life activities and insights that paint a picture of how your child demonstrates these developmental concepts**

1 Cognitive
Development

2 Social Emotional
Development

3 Language
Development

4 Creative
Development

5 Physical
Development

6 Health and Care

in everyday life. In addition to examples, there are tips and advice for parents and primary caregivers to use to support and guide you as you and your child encounter and master each of the upcoming milestones.

The Whole Child Parenting Program has developed five smart, modern, easy steps to help you raise a happy, thriving child.

> **The Whole Child Parenting Program involves:**
>
> 1. **Committing yourself**
> 2. **Educating yourself**
> 3. **Creating the right environment**
> 4. **Using the right materials**
> 5. **Staying on track**

That's it. Five steps to making your experience with your child the most rewarding and productive experience in your life.

STEP ONE: COMMITTING YOURSELF

Let's start with commitment. As a parent you have already taken the huge step of accepting responsibility for the little person in front of you. What is next required might not even be a step that needs articulating for you, but it bears repeating here: **You need to commit quality time to raising your whole child.**

There is no formula or script when it comes to being successful in parenting. Many parents look to doctors, textbooks, and experts for the secrets to parenting success. And while all of these are great sources, none address the whole child. And the whole child needs your attention.

Each child is different and has a different temperament, different interests, and a different personality. As a parent, you are also different. Every parent has different values that come from being a part of different cultures, socioeconomic classes, education levels, religions, and family sizes. The best way to be successful in parenting is to be involved with your child. By being involved and communicating with your child, you are better able to support her and her needs.

Many wonder what the real measures and outcomes of good parenting are. It does not involve your child having a high IQ, being talented in sports, or making a lot of money. Good parenting results in raising a child who grows up to give back to society, is independent, has a good work ethic, gets along well with others, and understands her identity and self-worth.

When it comes to measuring your success as a parent, it is important to look at the quality of the relationship you have with your child and not how effectively you can control your child. Just because your child listens and follows the rules does not mean she understands or respects them; it just means she is obedient.

The quality of your relationship has to do with your involvement and communication with your child. Know what guidelines are appropriate to set for your child, and explain them in a way that shows why these rules are necessary and important. As a parent, you need to meet your child's needs and help her feel respected. This can be done by explaining the reasons behind rules and discussing your child's feelings and opinions.

When your child feels like she is a valued member of the family and the community, she will then develop the confidence needed to begin moving toward being independent and making her own decisions.

Parents who are uninvolved with their children tend to make their children feel ignored and unvalued. At the same time, parents who are overly controlling and establish strict rules over all avenues of their children's lives tend to make their children feel stressed and have low self-esteem. It is important to find the middle ground between controlling your child and overlooking your child.

Your child is born naturally impulsive, immature, and ambitious, and she looks to you for guidance and support. This is why it is important to **make sure you communicate clear guidelines and expectations** for your child to alleviate stress and misunderstandings.

THE FOUR STYLES OF PARENTING

Whole Child Parenting: Age Two combines research, expert advice, and firsthand experience. In the past few decades, early childhood education has grown exponentially.

In the late 1950s, psychologist Erik Erikson organized development from birth to death into eight stages; according to Erikson, a person cannot successfully excel in the next stage of life without first completing the stage before.

Looking specifically at the first three stages, which cover ages birth to five, we see that a person's success lies first in his relationship with his parents. **Stage 1,** covering ages birth to two years old, focuses on a child's ability to develop **trust** with his parents. From there, children move on to **Stage 2** (for ages two to four years old), when the child is developing autonomy. **Autonomy** is your child's sense of self as an individual. Your child develops a sense of self by exploring the environment, learning about his own interests, and testing his limits. Moving forward to **Stage 3** (ages four to five years old), your child is **finding his purpose and place** within the family.

In the last 40 years, developmental psychologists have established **four styles of parenting.** The best parenting style is a combination of these four parenting styles—one in which you approach different situations with different solutions and always communicate with your child.

Authoritarian Parenting

The authoritarian parenting style can best be described as strict. Authoritarian parents tend to set rules that result in rewards or punishment if they are not followed. Rules are not explained and usually follow a reasoning of "because I said so." **These parents usually set high demands and expect obedience** but are not very responsive to their children. Children who grow up under the authoritarian parenting style tend to be obedient and usually well performing in school but socially exhibit signs of shame, low self-esteem, and lowered happiness levels.

Authoritative Parenting

The authoritative parenting style establishes rules and guidelines for children instead of just demands. Authoritative parents are more nurturing and forgiving, rather than simply punishing. They are responsive to their children and willing to listen and answer questions.

An important quality of authoritative parents is that they create clear standards for their children and adjust those standards based on their children's conduct.

Children who grow up under the authoritative parenting style tend to be capable and successful at learning new things. Socially and emotionally, they feel accepted and tend to be happy.

Permissive Parenting

The permissive parenting style is one that has few demands or guidelines. Parents tend to have low expectations for their children's maturity and abilities. **Permissive parents are more lenient with rules, preferring to avoid confrontation.**

This parenting style is usually nurturing and communicative but leaves children looking at their parent as more of a friend. Children who grow up under the permissive parenting style tend to often have poor self-regulation skills and may experience problems with authority and have trouble in school.

Uninvolved Parenting

The uninvolved parenting style is one with even fewer demands as well as little communication and responsiveness. Uninvolved parents fulfill their children's basic needs but tend to be detached and unavailable for their children in all other areas.

Children who grow up under the uninvolved parenting style tend to have low self-esteem, a hard time regulating their emotions, and a hard time making friends.

Your child's personality and temperament play a major role in how you choose your parenting style.

Research shows correlations

between parenting styles and their impact on children. There is also evidence showing other factors, such as a child's personality and the outside environment, playing a role as well. Your larger environment— such as culture, religion, socio-economic class, and family style— can also affect how your child reacts to your parenting. School, friends, and personality play a significant role in how your child responds to your parenting style.

It is important to be consistent with your parenting style, especially when it comes to discipline and setting expectations for your child. Besides taking into account her environment, think about other people in your child's life, such as your spouse or partner or caregiver. Take time to talk to each other about parenting styles and how you will work together when raising your child. Talk about what you both value as important and how you were each raised; this is important for keeping your parenting style consistent.

At the end of the day, you need to remember to be present and realistic. Be present both physically and mentally in order to be responsive to your child's needs. Be realistic in your expectations and the guidelines you set for your child.

Committing quality time as a parent, whichever parenting style(s) you choose, is the single most important factor in your child's healthy development.

STEP TWO: EDUCATING YOURSELF

Addressing the whole child means knowing about the general developmental milestones your child will experience at each age. Milestones define peak stages of accomplishment when your child achieves the end of one stage before moving on to the next. Milestones are exciting, because when a child reaches one you get to see how far she has come. And you get to look forward to the next amazing stage your whole child will go through.

But how can you be aware of milestones without knowing the specific developmental categories the stages occur in? How can you have realistic expectations about what is age appropriate and what your whole child should or should not be doing? *Whole Child Parenting: Age Two* lays out six major developmental areas of your child's growth and follows them through this year of your child's development.

Cognitive development

The first area of development is cognitive development. Cognitive development refers to the process of learning and the growth of intelligence and other mental capabilities, such as memory, reasoning, problem solving, and thinking. Memory and problem solving play a large role in your child's ability to engage in science, mathematical thinking, and logic.

Your involvement strengthens your child's cognitive abilities over these next years and plays a significant role in her school readiness and how she will learn and retain information later in life. At birth, your child's brain is only a quarter of the size of an adult brain; by age five, it has grown to be close to the same size and volume as yours.

Take advantage of these first five years to set the path and exercise the brain to its fullest potential. The Whole Child Parenting Program will very clearly define the stages of cognitive development and will help you be involved in your child's growth in this area.

Social-emotional development

Social-emotional skills reflect how effectively your child is able to interact in social settings. In order to interact well he must develop positive relationships. He must learn to recognize and regulate his emotions and reactions while communicating his feelings.

For young children, social-emotional skills provide a pivotal foundation upon which are built a range of other skills that are necessary in preschool as well as on play dates. Development in this category will help to determine how well your child succeeds with peer interaction throughout his life.

In order to interact well with others your child must develop positive relationships with others. He must also effectively coordinate his actions with communicating his feelings. As well, he must learn to recognize and regulate his emotions and reactions in many different social settings.

Your child needs to have good self-regulatory skills (i.e. the ability to calm himself down), keen emotional understanding (i.e. learning with help what made him feel the way he does), and growing communication skills such as naming how he feels and dealing with those feelings.

Language development

Language development is how your child communicates, from basic sounds and gestures to the use of pictures in books and words for speaking. As she ages your child will be communicating more than her emotions and needs. She will begin to tell stories, ask questions, and describe people and objects.

Your child will use memory to remember words and past events when telling stories. At an early age, your child's memory will also play a role in symbolic play when she uses props and objects as symbols to represent her ideas. These symbols will later translate to letter recognition and emerging literacy.

The Whole Child Parenting Program identifies how to use sign language to support early literacy skills, and we also include signs in supplemental and supportive materials in the program. Sign language for communication plays a role in your child's social-emotional development because it makes her better able to convey her emotions and needs when she is largely preverbal.

Creative development

Creative development involves how your child uses music, art, movement, and dramatic play to express himself and build imaginative thinking. When doing art, let your child make a mess and indulge in all the different textures and materials you provide. Make a paintbrush or other tools available to your child and then let him explore the paint with his hands.

Creative development plays a big role in your child's physical development as well. Music and movement build your child's gross motor skills (big muscles) by allowing your child to test balance and large body movements. Visual art builds your child's fine motor skills (small muscles) by allowing him to explore materials such as scissors, paintbrushes, and crayons.

Creative development can be used as an avenue for social-emotional development. Through art and dramatic play, your child can express and act out feelings, model behavior, or work through emotions.

Through activities, examples, and tips, *Whole Child Parenting: Age Two* shows how important creative development can be to your child's other areas of development as well.

Physical development

Physical development refers to your child's control over fine motor skills (small muscle movements of fingers, toes, and wrists) and gross motor skills (bigger movements that use the large muscles in the arms, legs, and torso). Between birth and five years old, your child's body and motor abilities make great strides. **Physical development has a lot to do with your child's self-esteem and sense of trust.** Your child is more willing to test her physical skills of throwing, kicking, and balancing when she feels comfortable and confident within her environment.

Physical development is important because it plays a large role in children developing independence and self-help skills. Getting dressed, feeding themselves, and cleaning up are all skills that involve both fine and gross motor skills, which, when combined, develop sensory motor skills.

The Whole Child Parenting Program explains how your child's physical changes correlate with the development of motor abilities and overall physical growth and development.

Health and care

This section discusses safety, grooming, self-help, and the health of your child. As your child grows older, he will be more independent with his hygiene, from small achievements like brushing his own teeth to bigger accomplishments like potty training.

As he goes through each developmental stage, your child's body is changing and growing at a swift pace. He is growing taller, sprouting new teeth, and becoming more active, which will reflect in changes in his diet each year.

Whole child parenting also involves using yoga. Yoga is a great resource in which to engage your child from infancy through age four and beyond. Not only does it allow your child to explore his balance, but it also strengthens his social-emotional development by helping him find an avenue to calm himself. Yoga can also provide a bonding experience for parent and child.

Reaching Milestones

An important and exciting addition to our exploration of the six developmental categories is the Reaching Milestones section we provide at the end of the book. This assessment list will allow you to see everything your child should be doing and accomplishing developmentally around that age. Milestone assessments provide an exciting reflection of all that you are doing to support your whole child.

STEP THREE: CREATING THE RIGHT ENVIRONMENT

Now that you have committed your time and started educating yourself, it is time to follow through by setting up the right environment. Setting up an environment where your whole child will thrive plays a large role in all six areas of their development.

The importance of play

We are in a day and age in which there is an abundance of technology and information available to us. It is hard to remember a time when an answer to a question wasn't a mouse click away or we couldn't watch a video about how to fix something.

Technology has made our lives so much easier over the years, but that is not the case when it comes to our little ones. Young children need to have the opportunity to make their own connections and discoveries within their environment. Children between the ages of birth and three learn the most through play.

When setting up an environment that fosters **free play**, it is important to have child-sized furniture as well as incorporate baskets and trays for storing toys. Child-sized furniture and organizational materials such as bins and trays for different categories of toys help your child build independence and self-help skills. Being able to pick what he wants to play with from the shelf or bin will build upon your child's personal interests.

Just because your child is more in control of what activity and materials he is exploring in free play does not mean that you do not need to be involved in free play with your child. Setting up learning and play environments and making learning materials available is just part of encouraging free play. When watching your child explore materials in free play, it is important to interact with him.

The main aspect to remember about free play is that your child's interests guide it.

Structured play is also an important type of play and can help foster and build specific skills. Structured play differs from free play based on the fact that you are planning the activity and materials in which your child is engaging. You are leading the way with a specific activity that has a specific goal. Examples of structured activities can be doing a science experiment with your child or sorting different colored blocks. It is important to have both a combination of structured and free play activities available for your child.

Indoor environments

Incorporating child-sized furniture as well as baskets and trays for storing toys helps your child build independence and self-help skills.

Trays and baskets allow you to provide more manipulatives (age appropriate toys that foster growth) for your child and make it easier for your child to help care for and clean her environment. **When furniture and materials are at your child's eye level, she is able to have better control of her physical movements and be more aware of her environment.**

When setting up an environment that is beneficial for your child's language skills, it is important to have age-appropriate books available. Your child's interest in books both while reading with you as well as pretending to read on her own helps her relate words to pictures. Take your child's language learning to the next level and place labels like TABLE on your kitchen table. Your child will start making the connection between words and objects.

When doing art, let your child get messy and indulge in all the different textures and materials you provide. Investing in an easel, putting down a tarp, providing a smock, or buying washable paint can help you make your indoor environment fit for creative exploration. Having some paper and crayons out on a table that is child-sized makes expressing herself and her ideas easy. She can use the crayons to express herself creatively and create symbols that depict her feelings or needs.

Besides art materials, your child can express her thoughts and feelings through dramatic play by modeling roles and situations when dressing up or using props. Having a mirror in your child's room allows her to explore her self-concept skills. You will find your child making different faces in the mirror or watching herself stack blocks. Having a mirror that is at your child's eye level builds her self-concept by developing a better understanding of herself as an individual who has her own interests and ideas. Don't overwhelm your child with too many choices or structured activities, but instead follow your child's needs and interests to help encourage independence.

Your commitment to your child is very important when it comes to building attention span and memory skills. Having a rug or a chair that is child-sized will make your child more comfortable and thus want to spend longer on an activity. Your child's attention span is a cognitive skill, and it grows as your child grows older.

The Whole Child Parenting Program provides you with all the guidelines, furniture, educational books, activities, supplies, and toys for your whole child's stimulating environment.

Outdoor environments

Environments where your child can engage in free play allow him to develop self-identity and develop his own interests. He is able to learn more about himself by testing his cognitive and physical limits. There aren't always many opportunities for your child to fully engage in free play at home, which is why **outdoor environments provide beneficial play spaces for your child.**

By its nature, play is flexible, changeable, and multifaceted, so your child's play environment should reflect those criteria as well. Play is a core and vital component of how young children learn. Structured and unstructured play provide health benefits by allowing your child to be physically active as well as engaging in problem-solving and creative exploration.

Outdoor environments provide space and opportunities for structured activities that help children learn to communicate and work together, while unstructured activities in large, open areas help your child push limits and take risks.

Your child can make a mess, climb, shout, jump, and run as fast as he wants in open spaces. He can fully express himself and explore his body's movements. From this, your child will develop a sense of competence and confidence in his own physical abilities.

Large, open areas provide opportunities for your child to be creative and use his imagination. He can make connections and witness vivid colors, patterns, and textures in an outdoor environment.

Without material items, media, or structured rules, children can create their own games, engage in dramatic play, and entertain themselves through the use of their mighty imagination.

Nature provides an abundance of science and math opportunities that your child can explore and manipulate. Problem solving, learning cause and effect, and investigating use all of your child's senses. Your child will be exposed to nature and its elements and make connections by witnessing weather, ecology, growth, and natural life cycles. He can explore what happens when he throws a rock in a pond, adds water to dirt or sand, or watches snow melt.

It is not always easy to find a safe outdoor environment for your child. For families in the city, it may mean you need to travel a little farther, but the benefits are worth it. Outdoor environments can actually be considered cleaner than indoor environments, especially when it comes to germs.

By being in a large space with richly fresh air, germs and infectious agents are spread out. Indoor spaces tend to be more enclosed, which leaves bacteria to sit on surfaces and linger. Overall, the benefits of outdoor environments are enormous, and you need to take advantage of them.

How you set up your child's indoor and outdoor environments plays a large role in how he learns and develops. It is important to remember that you are a part of his environment and in order for your child to thrive, he needs both a rich learning environment and your involvement.

STEP FOUR: USING THE RIGHT MATERIALS

As parents, we frequently buy and invest in products and toys that are not age appropriate and serve no purpose developmentally, which is why the Whole Child Parenting Program has created developmentally appropriate tools and materials for the whole child that are both fun and educational.

When starting the Whole Child Parenting Program from infancy, you are able to build and adjust your child's environment and learning materials as she grows older. Many materials, such as toys and furniture, are able to grow with your child from infancy to kindergarten. Other materials, such as Whole Child Parenting activity books, toys, and parent resources, assist you with staying on track with your child's development while also helping you plan and measure your time and commitment to your child. The Whole Child Parenting Program is here to walk with you through these first five years.

A variety and quantity of materials are needed to accommodate young children's short attention spans. Children learn through concrete activities, and parents must be able to provide activities for both their physical, active needs and calm, quiet needs.

Having the right environment with both active and quiet play can help your child's social-emotional development by encouraging self-regulating skills. Having a quiet area to go to when your child feels over-stimulated or needs a break is just as essential as having a safe area for her to be active and test her physical and creative limits.

A variety of materials is required

to stimulate the development of each age group. Some materials may fit into one or more categories; for example, an art activity can also serve as a fine motor exercise, and dramatic play can also act as a social-emotional tool.

It is important to remember that in order for your child to be able to explore and manipulate materials, she needs to have the materials made easily available to her at all times of the day. Setting up the right environment and investing in furniture that is both safe and easily accessible will play an important role in supporting your child's development.

STEP FIVE: STAYING ON TRACK

Once you have set up your environment, the Whole Child Parenting Program makes staying on track easier by providing you with activity books, toys, and learning materials. Consistency and routine play a big role in your whole child's development, so it is up to you to follow through and use these materials with your child.

Five years may seem far away, but time always has a way of sneaking up on us. In the blink of an eye, your child will be five years old and boarding the bus for school. This is a big milestone in your child's life, but you will be confident your child is ready for school because the Whole Child Parenting Program has helped you stay on track with your child's development. Your child is leaving for school a confident, happy, healthy learner.

In the end, all we want for our children is for them to be happy and confident because happiness and confidence set your child on the road to success. The Whole Child Parenting Program is here to get you to that point so you can take a deep breath and know your child is ready to face the world.

Through our *Whole Child Parenting: Age Two* book, educational materials, and workbooks, tips, and activities, apps, videos, and web support, you will have the tools to build a relationship with your child that allows him to confidently express himself through his creative and social-emotional skills, which in turn help him build his cognitive, language, and physical skills. You want your child to be healthy, happy, and complete, developing at or ahead of the curve. The Whole Child Parenting Program was developed for you, the committed and caring parent.

two >

Milestones for a Two Year Old

- Can do simple sorting
- Recognizes and names colors
- Sings parts of simple songs
- Recalls past experiences

SOCIAL-EMOTIONAL 2

- Shows independence and awareness of body parts
- Identifies and talks about personal feelings
- Shows interest in helping with basic tasks

 ## LANGUAGE 3

- Shows interest in books
- Puts together simple sentences
- Can talk about books
- Can tell own age
- Knows first and last name

 ## CREATIVE 4

- Believes stuffed animals are friends
- Plays with rhyming words
- Moves to music

 ## PHYSICAL 5

- Runs with ease
- Bends over easily
- Rides a tricycle
- Holds markers and crayons

 ## HEALTH AND CARE 6

- Almost all teeth in place
- Controls motor behaviors
- Body looks more proportional, longer legs and arms
- Potty trains, able to stay dry between potty times

two

Two year olds are thirsty for knowledge and are constantly exploring their environment and asking the question "Why?" They are starting to problem solve on their own, make connections, and categorize things based on color, shape, and size. This is an exciting time for your child in which you can introduce them to new languages, skills, and environments. Let's look at these milestones and more in the six areas of a two year old's development.

1. Cognitive Development

> Cognitive development refers to how your child's mind is working and his process of learning.

At two years old, your child's brain grows so fast that 250,000 nerve cells are added every minute. Your child's brain continues to grow after birth; by two years of age, your child's brain will be about 80% of the size of an adult brain.

In this year, your child's learning process is becoming more thoughtful and is greatly influenced by his environment. Your child is naturally curious and inquisitive and through his play investigates to make sense of the world around him.

During this stage of development, two year olds demonstrate how their minds are making more connections. Your child is moving past just observing and manipulating objects in his environment and is now beginning to understand the relationship between objects and ideas.

The following chart provides you with an image that walks you through the stages of your child's intellectual development.

Understanding these areas of cognitive development will help you learn how your child thinks, how to support learning, and how to teach new skills.

Pretend
Play

Attention
Span

Problem
Solving

Spatial
Relationships

Math and
Numbers

WHOLE CHILD: AGE TWO
Cognitive
Development Components

Under each cognitive area, the chart below gives you specific skills you can expect to see as your two year old develops. This chart will allow you to have practical expectations for your child at this age.

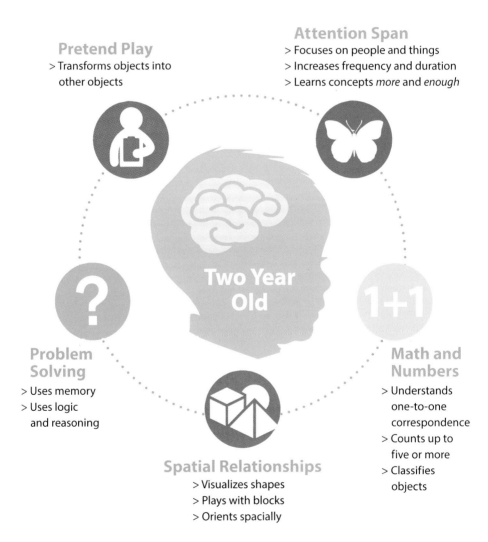

Pretend Play
> Transforms objects into other objects

Attention Span
> Focuses on people and things
> Increases frequency and duration
> Learns concepts *more* and *enough*

Two Year Old

Problem Solving
> Uses memory
> Uses logic and reasoning

Math and Numbers
> Understands one-to-one correspondence
> Counts up to five or more
> Classifies objects

Spatial Relationships
> Visualizes shapes
> Plays with blocks
> Orients spatially

Through his senses and developing motor skills, your child will use cause and effect and reasoning to explore unfamiliar objects. You will see your child start making connections between items and then begin organizing them into groups and categories.

Some of these connections can be seen through simple tasks such as sorting toys by color as well as through symbolic play, in which your child may use one object to represent another based on its physical features such as shape or size.

As parents, it is important to provide everyday activities that tap into your child's curiosity to help nourish the brain, which, in turn, will increase your child's learning efficiency and brain capacity. Any mental stimulation provided to your child will activate his mind and protect against cognitive decline.

You are preparing your child for the Olympics, and you have about five years to do it. This will feel like a lot of time, but in actuality, five years go by very quickly. Similar to the training of an athlete in the Olympics, the brain gets activated (warms up) and develops (refines skills) through repeated experience (workouts), interactions (team play), and environmental exposure (proper equipment and practice area), leading to greater performance.

Your child's brain is preparing for the Olympics as well, and in this case, the first five years are the most crucial for starting on the right path to developing your child's full potential.

The subsequent chapters show you how your child acquires knowledge and demonstrates major development in brain growth.

Attention Span >
All Eyes on You

Attention span refers to your child's ability to focus on a person and activity while ignoring other distracting things in the environment.

ACTIVITY

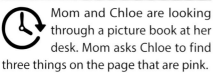 Mom and Chloe are looking through a picture book at her desk. Mom asks Chloe to find three things on the page that are pink.

Chloe points to a pink dress on the page and says, "Look, a pink dress!" but then loses focus and interest when it comes to finding two other pink items.

Mom notices this and says, "Chloe, why don't we find two more pink items before we turn the page?"

Chloe then looks at the page again and finds another pink item. "Good job!" Mom says as they turn to read the next page.

INSIGHT

With Mom's help, Chloe is able to focus on the activity of finding three pink items longer than if she had done the activity alone. Mom is realistic in offering Chloe a simple activity when she asks her to find the pink items and does not force her to pay attention longer than two minutes.

In order for your child to learn about or remember something, she must stop and pay attention.

You will see your child's attention span grow tremendously over this year of her life. At the beginning of age two your child's attention span for one single activity is only about 30–60 seconds, but with your encouragement and involvement can soon last between two to three minutes.

By two and a half, your child is becoming more independent, and you will see her able to focus on an activity independently for up to two minutes if the activity is of interest to her.

By doing the following as a parent you will support developing your child's attention skills so she can engage in focused play activities:

1.	2.	3.	4.
Be mindful of how your child is feeling and what mood she is in, because when your child is sad, unhappy, tired, cranky, or just not ready to do an activity, her ability to focus decreases and paying attention becomes more difficult.	Set up the environment in which your activity will take place.	Make sure the area is not disturbed by loud noises or distractions from a TV or other electronic devices.	Be mindful of frequent interruptions by others as this can cause your child to lose focus on the activity in front of her.

Following these four steps, coupled with having an activity that is of interest to your child will enable your child to develop better attention skills.

If your child becomes distracted, provide support by making face-to-face contact and saying your child's name out loud, then remind your child of the activity you are working on. Keep in mind that speaking slowly and calmly and praising your child for her efforts at paying attention is most effective for keeping her engaged.

Attention is a very important skill for your two year old to have, because it is the groundwork for future development of memory and intelligence; however, attention is a difficult skill for your child to acquire, so give her time.

By playing with your two year old and asking her questions about the activity, you are helping her apply and build her attention skills.

Math and Numbers >
Numbers Game

Math and number awareness involves your child recognizing numbers, counting, learning one-to-one correspondence, identifying patterns, and engaging in sorting and classifying.

Can you find all the spoons and put them together in one spot?

Math and number awareness is the foundation for learning more advanced math concepts.

Classification is putting together things that are the same. Your child demonstrates early classification skills by sorting items based on how they look, sound, and feel.

ACTIVITY

 Dad places a few plastic cups and spoons mixed together on the floor in front of Eric. Dad asks, "Eric, can you find all the spoons and put them together in one spot?" Eric begins to pick up one spoon at a time and place them next to each other. Next Dad asks, "Eric, can you now put all the cups together in one spot?" Eric begins to pick up a cup and put it next to another cup until they are all in one spot.

INSIGHT

Dad supports Eric's math awareness by having him find and classify objects that are the same. Once the child has mastered classification skills, you must then expand his mathematical thinking by talking about the differences between the groups of objects.

Your child is aware that things belong together because of what the object does or how objects are used. For example, when your child thinks about a birthday cake he will also think about having candles with the cake to celebrate. This is because both items are used when celebrating a birthday, even though a cake and candles do not look alike. This is classification.

Your child is able to identify when there is one object as well as when there is more than one object; however, while your child understands that there is more than one cracker on his plate, he will not yet be able to tell you if there are four or six crackers on that plate.

Your child can count up to three and maybe higher but not yet in the correct order. Your child will most likely count items in groups larger than two like this: "One, two, three, five, seven . . ." This is because your child understands through the skill of one-to-one correspondence that he can assign only one number to one object; however, he does not yet understand that the number he is assigning is related to the quantities of objects that he is naming.

Classifying skills are easy to support by doing activities as in the example with Eric, in which Dad uses simple materials found around the home, which Eric sees every day in his environment, or by helping the child see how items can be classified based upon how they are used, as in the example of the birthday cake.

Classifying objects is an important part of developing early math skills because it will help your child identify and describe relationships between objects. Your child's ability to classify objects he is playing with supports math skills such as understanding one-to-one correspondence.

It is important that your child can touch the items while counting so that each item represents a number. Children learn math skills best through hands-on play and the use of concrete examples using blocks, toys, or other household items.

Understanding number relationships and the purpose of numbers in counting leads your child to later be able to recognize patterns in materials and objects around him as well as patterns in his daily routine, such as the notion that naptime comes after lunch time. Patterns, routines, daily activities all lead to building math skills.

ACTIVITY

 Ben is playing with blocks on the floor of his bedroom. He starts to count out the amount of blocks he has in front of him by grabbing and moving one block at a time toward his body.

Ben says, "One block" and then moves one block. Then he says, "Two blocks" and moves another block. When Ben moves a third block next to the others he says, "Three blocks."

"One block.
Two blocks.
Three blocks."

INSIGHT

By counting and moving the blocks toward him, Ben is learning one-to-one correspondence, which is when each block represents a number. Later he will learn the symbol for the numbers: 1, 2, and 3.

Counting skills are best learned when the child has an opportunity to touch and feel, sort and categorize objects or toys.

Remember, the Whole Child Parenting Program offers appropriate developmental products and monthly activity books that walk you through supporting your child's skills. Using these in conjunction with the recommended age-appropriate room materials ensures faster development.

Spatial Relationships >
Shape, Size, Distance

Spatial relationships refer to location and where things are in the environment (*on top*, *under*, *beside*, *next to*, *inside*, *outside*). When she understands these concepts she can better understand the concepts of distance and directions she is given.

Two year olds are more independent compared to toddlers, and their use of spatial skills has improved and will continue to improve as they grow. This is demonstrated by your child's ability to maintain her body in relation to her surrounding environment. Parents must support their child's spatial development by giving **spatial cues**.

ACTIVITY

Tommy's mom places a large refrigerator box on the living room floor. Tommy and Laura begin to move around inside the box, turning their bodies in different directions until they both are able to fit inside.

INSIGHT

Children understand and develop the concept of *inside* by moving around within the confines of the rectangular shape and work together to use available space in a fun, entertaining, and satisfying way.

Which shape is a circle?

ACTIVITY

Jasmine is having a picnic lunch outside with her mom. Mom places an O-shaped cereal piece and a cracker in front of Jasmine and asks her what shapes she can see.

Jasmine is able to point to the O-shaped cereal and say it is a circle and that the cracker is a square.

INSIGHT

Jasmine is able to identify the circle and the square shapes based on their visual qualities, such as curved and straight lines. When Jasmine gets closer to age three, she will be able to articulate to Mom how many sides a square has and see that a circle does not have any sides. This skill forms an early basis for understanding simple geometry (identifying angles and shapes).

Spatial cues might include parents asking their child to find two of the same things in the environment, such as asking your two year old to "Get the ball under the table" (spatial cue of where the ball is located), as opposed to "Get the ball" (no cue is given as to where the ball is located). Spatial cues encourage your child to use primarily the sense of sight to focus on the sizes and shapes of the objects she is looking for in the environment (e.g. ball [shape], under table [size]).

Your child's spatial ability with shapes is purely visual. Children visualize and can see similarities and differences in shapes (straight, curved, zig-zagged, looped, thick, thin, circle, triangle, square, rectangle, flat, and pointy). Spatial abilities develop with time and experience.

Shapes are everywhere. As in the example with Jasmine, you are able to see how your child has shapes all around her. Therefore, the more you engage your child in spatial play by talking about shapes, the better chance your child will have of building the foundations necessary for other early math skills.

Problem Solving >
Keep Trying

Your child is naturally curious. Through active exploration he will use trial and error to figure out a problem.

When you think about the role memory plays in problem solving for your child, you will see him observe, think about a problem, and then later remember what he saw someone else do and imitate it.

Through everyday routines, parents can provide opportunities for their children's memories to improve. When getting ready for the bath, encourage your child to recall what is needed to take a bath. This will encourage your child to think about what to do if he doesn't have items necessary for taking a bath.

Your child is also starting to understand the relationship between objects, and you will see your child exploring this through cause and effect. As your child's understanding

---

ACTIVITY

 Max is given two toy connectors to play with. He sits for a moment looking at both connectors, trying to figure out how they fit together to make a tower. After a few minutes, Max remembers that he can put one connector on top of the other, and he continues that process with other connectors to make a tower.

INSIGHT

In this example, Max uses trial and error to figure out how to fit the connectors together and then uses his memory to follow the same process with the rest of the connectors.

As he learns new information his brain will reorganize itself and store knowledge in the memory bank for later use with solving problems that occur through other play activities.

of cause and effect develops, he will express interest in pushing buttons and turning light switches on and off to see what happens.

You will see your child explore cause and effect situations all around him. One example is your child interacting with a family cat using a cat toy, a ball attached at one end to a string.

To see a cause, your child needs to think about how to produce the action needed to get a response from the cat (should he move the cat toy up or down, fast or slowly?). Your child will see the effect of bouncing the toy in front of the cat's face.

Activities like simple interactions with a family pet enable your child's brain to absorb knowledge and grow. It is important to expose your two year old to a variety of stimuli and

allow him to have hands-on inter-action with different materials.

In other words, two year olds need sensory rich activities because when your child is able to both see and touch the objects he is exploring, he will make a deeper connection and develop a better understanding of concepts like cause and effect.

Your child's learning process has become more thoughtful and goes beyond just manipulating objects physically. This is why it is important to provide your child with the high-quality toys (which does not have to mean expensive) that are important to his learning processes.

As you think about buying toys, here are some examples that encourage a two year old's problem solving abilities:

- **Wood puzzles** (with four to twelve pieces) are excellent because your child has to really think about where the pieces fit.

- Find **blocks** that snap together encourage your two year old to think about how to fit them.

- Use **objects that can be sorted** (by size, shape, color, smell) and things with hooks, buttons, buckles, and snaps.

Pretend Play >
Model Behavior

Your two year old will begin to engage in more complex forms of pretend play.

ACTIVITY

Lila finds a banana in the kitchen and decides that she will go sit by her dad on the floor and pretend to talk, using the banana as a phone.

Because your child is now beginning to form mental images of objects, actions, and concepts he is able to put together and act out more elaborate sequences of pretend play.

One form of pretend play you will see your child engage in is symbolic play. Symbolic play is your child's ability to use objects, actions, or ideas to represent other objects, actions, or ideas.

Another form of pretend play your child engages in is socio-dramatic play. **Socio-dramatic play** appears at the time your child begins looking for the company of others. Socio-dramatic play includes elements of

INSIGHT

This is an example of symbolic play because Lila is using an object, the banana, to represent a real object, which is a phone. Lily is also able to understand that a phone is used to communicate and talk to others.

Your child is showing you how she is categorizing objects based on how they look. The banana has a similar shape to a phone. Another example is a pot being used as a hat because both items have a similar shape and features.

Symbolic play is important because through play your child will express and represent his ideas, thoughts, and feelings.

"*How do you feel?*"

symbolic play; however, socio-dramatic play differs from symbolic play because it requires verbal interaction between two or more children.

Socio-dramatic play contributes to your child's ability to play with other children his age. As your child is engaged in play he is growing his vocabulary and developing conversation skills needed to engage in role playing events during play (e.g. you be the doctor, and I will be the one who is sick).

Socio-dramatic play gives your child something to talk about with another child or family member. Think about a play exchange your child had with you in which you were the patient and he was the doctor. You were asked by your child, "How do you feel?" and "Are you sick?" These types of experiences require listening and talking as well as giving a response.

A shared experience like this through socio-dramatic play supports the development of skills needed for the social interactions your child will encounter each and every day.

ACTIVITY

Teach your child to engage in make-believe play by setting up an environment that enables you to become your child's play partner. Play a game of doctor with your child, and have your child act out an experience he had with the doctor. Then switch roles so that he is the doctor and you are the patient.

INSIGHT

With your support, your child can overcome the anxiety he may have been experiencing regarding a doctor's visit. Practicing or rehearsing the sequence of events experienced on a typical visit to the doctor or other potentially stressful situations helps two year olds feel more comfortable and learn coping strategies (e.g. familiarity) for managing the situation.

2. Social-Emotional Development

> **Social-emotional development is the start of a two year old's knowledge, understanding, expression, and management of her emotions.**

Your two year old is building an understanding of herself as an individual, which increases her confidence in interacting with people, objects, and experiences in the world around her.

Healthy social and emotional development begins with your child having an attachment to other human beings. It is important that your two year old feels loved, important, and worthy. Because of that bond with you, she trusts that the world is a good place. These early relationships form the basis for all other relationships and interactions that she will have.

You will see your child develop an interest in playing with other children. Through interactions with other children, your child will begin to learn about empathy and others' feelings. Developing empathy enables her to cooperate and negotiate with her peers.

At this age your child has better control of her body and emotions because she is able to retain focus and attention longer. Your child's ability to control her emotions and refrain from acting on her first impulse also helps her co-operate and develop the ability to wait her turn and not grab toys from friends.

Self-Awareness

Social Development

Self-Regulation

Emotional Development

WHOLE CHILD: AGE TWO
Social-Emotional Development Components

Social-emotional development is the foundation for all other areas of development, because in order for your child to be a confident and attentive learner, she must first feel safe and valued.

1. Social Development

Social development is your child's ability to connect with fellow friends and adults in a socially acceptable way. This connection forms the foundation for two year olds to have healthy relationships with others and fit into social environments both now and in the future.

2. Emotional Development

Emotional development is the start of a two year old's knowledge, understanding, expression, and management of her feelings. Emotional development does not happen without connection to other people or things; the nervous system, cognition, and regulating behaviors are involved in emotional development.

3. Self-Regulation

Self-regulation involves a two year old's capability to gain control of her body, control strong emotions, and retain focus and attention. The development of self-regulation is the foundation of early childhood development.

4. Self-Awareness

Self-awareness in two year olds is seen when they begin to recognize themselves in mirrors, react by giving a self-conscious grin, or display shyness when they are the center of others' attention. Two year olds build their understanding of themselves as individuals, which increases their confidence in interacting with people, objects, and experiences in the world around them.

Healthy social and emotional development begins with your child having an attachment to other human beings.

Social Development >

Can I Play?

Social skill development occurs when your child understands the feelings of others and can create positive relationships with peers and adults.

"I have pizza for you!"

When your child was an infant, he engaged in solitary play (playing alone). When your child was a toddler, he engaged in both solitary play and parallel play (playing beside other children rather than with them). During both forms of play, your child was only interested in what he was doing.

Now your child wants to experience what it is like to really have a relationship with a peer whom they may later call a best friend. Your child's social skills have developed so much that associative play is what he wants to do.

Associative play is when children play together.

Your child's cooperation with other children grows as he develops more empathy regarding others' feelings and wants.

Two year olds will borrow from peers and share toys, but this does not mean that they will necessarily play cooperatively. When children turn three, you will see more cooperative play experiences take place.

ACTIVITY

 Two-and-a-half-year-old Josie is playing with her peer, Thomas, during morning playgroup. Josie spots a bin with colored blocks near Thomas and picks it up. One by one she takes out the blocks and lays them on the table in the shape of a circle. Josie calls out to Thomas, "Thomas, want some pizza? I have pizza for you!"

Thomas replies, "Yes, I want pizza. I don't like pepperoni pizza. It's spicy."

Josie replies, "It's cheese." She then grabs a small toy shovel from the sand table across the room and comes back to scoop up a block "slice" of pizza for Thomas. "Here's your pizza, Thomas!"

Thomas scoots over to Josie and then says, "I don't want cheese pizza!"

Josie starts to cry and says, "I have your pizza."

Thomas looks up and says, "Okay, pizza please, thank you."

As your child grows older it is amazing to see how he learns to cooperate more with another person through the use of verbal interaction and understanding that relationship building involves give and take.

It is important for your child to be able to interact with others in a positive way because this skill will support him well into adulthood. Interacting well includes your child being able to cooperate, communicate, and work through problems that can and will happen during ordinary play with peers.

Every stride your child makes in social development brings him closer to forming healthy, positive relationships with you and others in his environment. Support opportunities for him to engage with others on a regular basis.

INSIGHT

Thomas is able to see that Josie is upset, shows empathy, and decides to have the pizza. Both children demonstrate cooperation and relationship building skills.

Emotional Development >
Feelings

Emotional development refers to how your child understands her own feelings, as well as how she can read the feelings of others.

Because your two year old has a better understanding of her feelings, she will be able to respond when you ask questions like "Are you happy or sad today?" or "Why are you happy?" or "Why are you sad?" When your child is able to communicate her feelings, it gives you the opportunity to respond appropriately to her wants and needs.

Your child's emotional security and confidence develop when parents give warm, consistent, responsive care to their children. Part of showing warm and caring behavior to your two year old is being attentive and in tune with her feelings. Demonstrating this behavior shows your child how to use kind, caring, appropriate behavior when dealing with others.

ACTIVITY

Stephanie is sitting with her mom and reading a book. Her brother Leo has a play date with his friend Erik. The boys are playing in the other room.

Suddenly Stephanie hears loud noises. She runs into the living room where she sees Erik and Leo face to face. They are talking loudly and gesturing. It looks to her as if they are fighting.

She runs back to her mom and cries out, "Mommy, look!" and points to the boys in the other room.

Mom smiles at Stephanie and says, "It's okay, honey. The boys are pretending to be like two superheroes on TV who were comparing powers."

Stephanie calms down.

"It's nice that you were worried about your brother and his friend," Mom adds.

As Stephanie sees the smile on her mom's face, she begins to smile, too.

INSIGHT

Stephanie looks to her mother for directions when trying to figure out how to react. Stephanie is able to read her mother's emotions, hear her words, and act appropriately.

Having the ability to read the emotions of others is an important social skill that two year olds are beginning to develop. As they learn how to read others' emotions and react appropriately, children often look to their parents for directions when trying to figure out how to behave in certain situations.

As your child grows older she will look less to you for understanding someone else's emotions and decide for herself how the other person is feeling. She will begin to understand when she is making her friends happy or sad, when to give space, and when her friends need a hug. In other words, she will start becoming more emotionally intelligent over time and with more experience with family and peers.

It is important to praise your two year old's successes and show your child that you see how she is growing and learning. This will help build her confidence so she can have more success making friends.

Self-Regulation >
Emotions

Self-regulation is the ability to control one's own behaviors and expression of emotions.

Parents can be overwhelmed by emotions, but over time we have learned some strategies to help us regain control. Strategies could include taking a moment to count to ten or calling a friend to talk about your frustrations. But when your child has such feelings, he is not yet able to use the same coping or self-regulating mechanisms.

Self-regulation is demonstrated by your child's ability not to act upon his first response. You will see your child use self-regulating strategies such as calming himself by sucking his thumb, tolerating waiting minutes for his turn, sitting and focusing on a book being read to him, or refraining from hitting another child who has moved into his space.

There will always be a time when your child does not like to hear the word *no*. It is important to take a moment and look at the situation from your child's perspective. Then ask yourself if you are expecting your child to understand or do something when he is tired or does not understand what is being asked of him. Are you giving your child time to calm himself down (waiting before you react)? And have you been teaching your child the skills he needs to calm down on his own (holding a beloved toy, sitting for a little bit)?

If the answer is no and you still require your child to accept your request then you are forcing obedience through control; this is not being supportive, and it will delay the development of his self-regulation skills.

In addition, **it is imperative that parents are also modeling self-regulating behaviors so that the child can imitate, practice, and internalize what is being modeled for him.** Self-regulation is the cornerstone of your child's social-emotional development and will be seen in all areas of development as your child matures.

ACTIVITY

 Mom needs to go to the grocery store because she has run out of formula for Tony's baby sister. Mom knows Tony has not had his nap today, but she still has to go.

Arriving at the grocery store Mom puts the baby in the cart and has Tony hold onto the side of the cart. Then off they go toward the infant aisle.

Walking through the aisles Tony sees the candy section and begins to grab a bag of candy off the bottom shelf. Mom says, "Tony, no candy. Put it back, please."

At the moment Mom says no, Tony throws himself and the bag of candy on the floor and begins kicking and screaming, "I want candy!"

Mom remembers that Tony has not had his full nap and says, "I know you're upset. I'll wait for you to calm down." Mom then hands Tony his little blanket out of the diaper bag.

INSIGHT

Tony's mom understands that Tony has not had a nap, so she gives him some time before she reacts to his tantrum. She also gives Tony his blanket, which serves as a comfort item he can use to help himself calm down. Tony's mom has realistic expectations and also provides support for her two-year-old son.

Self-regulation skills develop slowly over time; this is why it is important for parents to have realistic expectations of their children.

Self-Awareness >

My Identity

Self-awareness in two year olds means having a clear and positive sense of identity.

Your child is starting to identify herself as an individual who has her own body, thoughts, and feelings separate from those of others.

In your child's search for self-identity, she is eager to use her mind, have her say, and make decisions. Saying "I don't want to" or "Not those shoes. I want pink shoes, pink!" is normal behavior for two year olds. When you say, "Yes," they say, "No."

She wants to choose what she wears, so let her! Lay out three outfits and let her pick one from those choices. Then say, "You can choose from these or I can choose for you." This gives your child a sense of control over her own destiny. It can be tough to get a particularly stubborn child on board, but decisions need to be made, so why not enlist her help?

It really speaks to your child's self-esteem that she is developing

ACTIVITY

 Katy stands in front of a mirror, looking at her face. She points to her nose and then points to the nose in the mirror.

INSIGHT

 Katy realizes that the face in the mirror is hers. Katy is becoming aware of what she looks like. This is how a child first begins to see herself as an individual, separate from others.

into an individual who is separate from you. Your two year old is experiencing a very important stage in her development. **In order for your two year old to become a healthy, thriving adult, she must separate from you, and now is the time she will start doing this.** Don't panic. She's not going far!

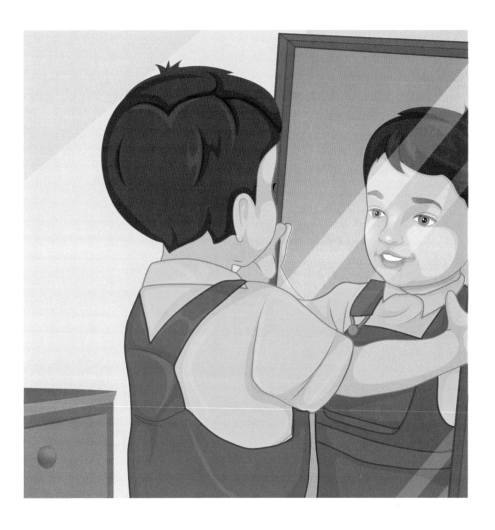

Developing a sense of self as a unique being starts with recognizing superficial features and characteristics.

3. Language Development

> **Language development encompasses your child's emerging reading and writing skills as well as the development of her communication skills, such as listening and speaking.**

Two year olds typically have a vocabulary of between 70 and 225 different words. Your child will develop language more swiftly if you and other adults engage her in real conversations.

Language development improves social-emotional, cognitive, and physical skills. Your child understands and uses language to communicate successfully with others, build relationships, and express her needs in multiple ways.

Your two year old is learning language by making connections between the words she hears and the meanings of these words. She is now able to put together words to form short sentences and phrases.

And while it may be quicker for your child to express herself verbally, sign language can serve as a great outlet for your child to communicate not just her needs but also her feelings.

As you support your two year old's familiarity with storybooks, you will also increase her expressive vocabulary skills and early reading abilities.

Listening and
Understanding

Emerging
Literacy

Communication
and Speaking

WHOLE CHILD: AGE TWO
Language
Development Components

Besides having storybooks available, there are a number of ways you can create a home environment that promotes emerging literacy for your child, such as labeling objects around the house to expose your child to more print and promote future skills like letter recognition.

Your support is key when it comes to your child's love for written and spoken words, transforming your child into a critical thinker and effective communicator.

1. Listening and Understanding

Two year olds learn language by making connections between the words they hear and the meanings of these words. These connections between words enable your child to put together words to form phrases and make different words from a root word; for example, the root word *appear* helps your child make sense of the words *disappear* and *reappear*.

2. Communication and Speaking

Two year olds use sounds, gestures, and words to have their needs met. They are building their vocabulary and are able to use two- and three-word phrases to communicate with others.

3. Emerging Literacy

Two year olds are able to recognize and identify almost all common pictures and objects around them. They are developing story comprehension as well as engaging in more conversations with others. This is what is called emerging or emergent literacy.

"Reading" and being read to are some of the most powerful ways to develop cognitive and language skills.

Remember, the Whole Child Parenting Program offers appropriate developmental products and monthly activity books that walk you through supporting your child's skills. Using these in conjunction with the recommended age-appropriate room materials ensures faster development.

Listening and Understanding >

Bit by Bit

Receptive language is the aspect of communication that involves hearing, listening, and understanding. In other words, receptive language skills involve the ability to understand words and language by hearing and listening.

"Can you say bear?"

Your child saying the wrong word is a normal part of the language development process. Often your child is saying the word wrongly because he did not hear the correct way of saying the word or because he did not understand the meaning of the word. Demonstrate the correct way to say a word and repeat with him many times. Use the word in context if you can (e.g. "Bears have fur. Do you see the bear's fur? Can you touch the bear's fur?") By repetition and with your support your child will be able to speak words correctly.

Receptive language is important in order for your child to communicate. Think about a time when your child had difficulty understanding something you asked him to do; having difficulty following directions often occurs because the child does not understand one of the words you are using.

When your child is able to understand directions and what is happening around him, he will be better able to pay attention and listen. Thus, having a good understanding of language will also make it easier for your child to engage in learning activities.

It is important that when you hear your child use a word wrongly, gently pronounce the word the correct way and have him repeat it back to you. Refrain from saying, "No, you said it

ACTIVITY

 Two-year-old Aaron is sitting with his mom at the table looking at a picture book about bears. He points to a picture of a bear and says, "That's a bar." (bear)

Mom responds, "Yes, that is a bear. Can you say bear?" (Here she is making sure she correctly says the word *bear* for her son and has him repeat the word.) "Good job! Now can you point to the bear?"

INSIGHT

By having Aaron repeat the word and find the pictures of the bear on the page, his mom is listening to hear how well her son hears the correct pronunciation and how well he understands what the word is. At this age your child mispronounces many words.

wrong" because that can discourage your child from trying again. Young children listen a lot! They listen to the sounds you make and the words and phrases you say. As your child develops more language and uses his receptive language skills, he will become more advanced in listening to and understanding information.

That is why it is important to give your child plenty of opportunities to develop his listening and understanding skills. After you have talked about a routine, follow up by asking your child if he can tell you what comes after breakfast or after hearing soft music or after a bath.

As your child listens and understands others, he is also learning that communication is important and useful in his everyday life.

Listening and understanding skills will play key roles in how your child communicates his feelings and how he interacts with others.

Opportunities can include:

1. talking during daily routines (e.g. "After breakfast we are going to brush our teeth.").

2. talking with your child about things that you are doing (e.g. "I am going to add eggs to the batter for our cookies.").

3. talking about things they can see in their environment (e.g. "I see a blue bird on the tree. He is building a nest.").

Communication and Speaking >

My Turn to Talk

Communication and speaking are how your child uses language to connect with others through avenues such as his voice to make sounds and his hands to sign words.

ACTIVITY

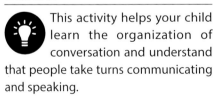

Mom makes a play telephone out of two empty cans and a piece of string for Tony and his neighbor to play with. Tony picks up the can on one side of the play telephone and says, "Nicole, can you hear me?"

Nicole says, "Tony, is that you?"

Both Tony and Nicole start laughing as they listen to the other speak through the can.

INSIGHT

This activity helps your child learn the organization of conversation and understand that people take turns communicating and speaking.

Be an interactive language partner with your child so that you are helping him learn to use language to communicate. When your child asks for something, respond appropriately, and he will begin to understand that exchanging information back and forth is an effective way of communication.

Describe how things taste, what they feel like, and how they smell. Speak with your child and ask him to reply—this will support the development of communication skills.

You should use two- or three-word phrases when speaking with your child. By the time your child reaches two, he should know and use 200 or more words when speaking.

It is important to stay in tune with your child's language communication and to talk often with him using a rich and varied vocabulary. The number of different words and phrases you use on a daily basis, as well as the number of conversations you have with your child, are both directly related to your child's language development. So keep up the talking!

Sign Language

Sign language is a form of communication used as your child combines hand and body movements to make words.

Mia is signing milk.

Your child is naturally drawn to speaking because it is the fastest and easiest way for her to communicate with others; however, during this age it is still difficult for your child to express exactly how she is feeling, especially during times of stress. That is because her vocabulary is still developing, and she is in the process of learning to pronounce words heard in his environment. Starting with simple signs, such as *happy* or *sad*, can give your child another way to express how she feels without using spoken language.

The other wonderful aspect of sign language is that your child will see it as fun. You use it as a way to support your child's language skills as you teach the signs for words and the alphabet. By teaching signs you are helping your child with letter recognition and vocabulary building.

In addition, teaching your child to use sign language as another outlet for communicating helps your child feel confident to "speak" her wants, needs, and feelings.

When you are able to understand her needs and be responsive, you are supporting your child's emotional development, which is crucial for developing self-esteem and the ability to learn.

Emergent Literacy >
The Written Word

"Can we taste with our nose?"

Emerging or emergent literacy relates to the development of knowledge and skills associated with books and writing.

It is your child's experience with reading and writing skills before she learns how to read and write words. Emergent literacy involves your child in the process of becoming literate.

ACTIVITY

Mother and daughter are reading a book titled *Silly Ways We Use Our Senses*.

Mom says, "It is so sweet to taste the lemon drop on the tree. We taste it with our nose. . . ." Mom pauses and repeats, "With our nose? Can we taste with our nose?"

Peyton says, laughing, "No! We taste with our mouth, not our nose."

Peyton then pretends to lick the lemon drops off the tree on the page, and her mom joins in.

INSIGHT

We see that Peyton's mom does not give directions to show Peyton that we do not taste with our noses when reading the story to her, but rather she gives assistance. Peyton's mom also joins in when Peyton decides to expand the story by using pretend play and creative movement.

Picture book reading and story reading should be one of the most common forms of interaction that occur between you and your child. While reading to your child point out different words to help her make connections between the print and the pictures.

It is important to remember that emergent literacy begins at home. Two year olds who live in a home environment that includes lots of reading and writing will develop reading and writing skills before they start school.

As she understands her environment, your two year old will select and focus on important aspects of literacy, one of which is written language. Two year olds are immersed in written language. They see books, newspapers, magazines, and words on screen. Parents must show their children that reading, writing, and talking about words occurs in everyday life and serves different purposes. Immersion in reading and writing will help your child develop a love of learning that can last a lifetime.

Create a supportive environment for your two year old's emergent literacy development. You can do this by trying the following:

1. Read as much as possible to your child and have many books available for your child to look through and pretend to read as she flips the pages.

2. Allow your child to explore with tools for writing and drawing (such as pencils and crayons).

3. Make simple labels in your child's room. For example, label the drawer where your child puts her socks by writing the word SOCKS on white paper or on an index card in large, black, capital letters.

4. Talk with your child about writing. When you write something down, draw her attention to it. Say things such as "I am leaving a note so they know where we went."

4. Creative Development

> Creative arts engage two year olds' minds and senses.

Creative arts invite your child to listen, observe, move, solve problems, and imagine—all while using multiple modes of thought and self-expression. By actively involving your child in the creative arts, you are stimulating brain connections that support learning.

You may find your two year old now claps to a basic musical beat, experiments with mixing colors to make a new color, or moves like the animal characters in a story.

This year, your child is taking on a greater interest in music and Is able to memorize words to her favorite songs. She will also start experimenting more with different dance movements. Her movements will start reflecting the beat, rhythm, and mood of the music. She can express herself while also strengthening her gross motor skills and exploring spatial relationships in her environment.

Your child will develop an interest in visual arts as she doesn't just explore art mediums and materials, but also starts to express herself by describing and discussing her art. Visual arts can include a limitless number of materials, which give your child infinite ways to express herself and explore her environment.

WHOLE CHILD: AGE TWO
Creative
Development Components

You will also see your child gravitate toward expressing herself through dramatic play. Through dramatic play your child is able to use her imagination to explore different roles, while also having an outlet to express her feelings by acting out familiar situations.

Each of these elements supports your child's imaginative thinking and self-expression, enhancing her progress in other areas of growth such as problem solving and emotional development.

1. Music

Music and words have a great connection for two year olds. Ask your child to sing her favorite song, and then sing it back to her. Repetition is key in early childhood learning. This is the age when children start to clearly use words to communicate needs and wants.

2. Dance

Two year olds move more freely than during the toddler stage. They are aware of their body parts and the reactions their movements make. They love to run and fall on the ground. Play games to encourage their understanding of moving slowly or quickly.

**Remember,
the Whole Child
Parenting Program**
offers appropriate developmental
products and monthly activity books
that walk you through supporting
your child's skills. Using these in
conjunction with the recommended
age-appropriate room
materials ensures faster
development.

3. Visual Arts

Two-year-old art is messy and hands-on. At this age, you might start to see the beginning stages of a story as your child draws. Ask your child what a line or form represents in her picture.

4. Dramatic Play

Two year olds get extremely excited by dress up and dramatic play. They combine their imagination and memory skills to express their thoughts and feelings. Objects have more meaning and are specifically chosen during dramatic play at this age.

Music >
I Got Rhythm

Music is sound that expresses ideas of emotions through rhythm, melody, and harmony.

Let's play these drums.

Musical experiences for two year olds involve listening to, learning about, and making music.

Music calms your little one during rest time. It also promotes listening skills. Through music your child will learn about patterns, and through singing your child will learn about language and rhymes. **When your child is between the ages of one and three, he will look for opportunities to get rocking, rolling, clapping, and moving to a beat.**

It is important for you to have resources available whereby you can enhance your child's musical opportunities. Part of supporting your child in music is giving opportunities for him to not only listen to music, but also to become actively engaged in it by playing an instrument along with the music, making his own music, dancing with music, and play acting with music.

ACTIVITY

Dad wants to give his son an opportunity to listen and play music with him. He goes to the garage and gets his small drums and two wooden drumsticks from when he was young.

Dad says, "Mark, come sit with me on the floor and let's play these drums I got from the garage." Dad hands the sticks to Mark and then turns on the piano concerto "Andante" by Mozart and begins to beat on the drums slowly with his hands.

Dad turns to Mark and says, "Mark, hit your drums like this, fast and then slowly like the music."

INSIGHT

Dad encourages Mark to bang out a rhythm and to imitate with his sticks what Dad is doing with his hands. As Mark continues to bang on the drums, he is also learning to keep a steady beat and coordinate his movements with the sticks in both hands.

Dance >
Moving

Dance is anytime your child moves to the rhythms of the sounds he hears.

Dance can be a sway, a twirl, or a jiggle. Dance can be fast or it can be slow, but most of all dance is movement.

Your child is learning about himself and the world around him through movement. Playing your child's favorite music and encouraging him to dance and play supports gross motor skill (large muscle) development and spatial exploration as your child moves in the space around him.

Movement includes exploration, experimentation, and discovery. Dancing helps your child explore all the new ways his body can move, such as using the large muscles of the body like his arms and legs to do a twist and a turn, a leap or a shimmy. Remember, dance is an art form, and when combined with the child dancing freely to the music (without following the moves of an adult) it will promote creativity and self-expression.

Visual Arts >
Little Artist

Visual arts can be experienced by your child using her sense of sight.

Art forms such as drawing, painting, crafts, pictures, and videos are all visual arts.

Your child can use materials such as crayons, paint, play dough, clay, glue, tape, paper, and everyday objects found around the house, along with tools such as child-safe scissors, brushes, rolling pins, and cookie cutters to express her ideas.

Visual arts benefit growth in all areas of your child's development. When your child describes what she has created she's using language. When your child uses cause and effect to see what happens when she combines two colors of paint she is developing her problem-solving skills.

It is important to enable your child to express her own ideas through the visual arts. Think of ways you can nurture her creativity and self ex-pression by letting her choose paint and crayon colors, asking questions about the colors she chooses, and discussing how she feels when she is painting or coloring a picture.

By playing an active role and praising your child's art, you are allowing her to feel confident to continue to express herself through further visual arts activities.

ACTIVITY

Molly's mom asks her if she wants to paint today. Very excitedly Molly says, "Yes!"

Mom gets a plain piece of white paper from the home office and tapes it to Molly's easel. Then Mom goes and gets a cup with blue paint and a paper towel roll and places them on the easel tray.

"Here you go, Molly," Mom says as she takes the paper towel roll and dips one end of it in the blue paint before handing it to Molly. Molly then begins to bang it on the paper, moving from left to right. "Mommy! Look! I made flowers!" Molly says.

"I love your flowers! They are so blue. Good job," Mom says.

INSIGHT

Mom gives Molly a chance to create any kind of picture she wants using paint. When she is done Mom does not ask Molly "What is it?" but instead waits for Molly to tell her and then praises her.

Dramatic Play >
Imitation Game

Dramatic play involves children taking on assigned roles and acting them out.

This is a time when your child will pretend to be a baker, doctor, or fire fighter with another peer or an adult.

The wonderful aspect of dramatic play is that it is spontaneous. You are able to see how your child perceives herself and the world when you watch her use her imagination to act out different roles and situations. Often your child will create a scene that is familiar or imitate family members. Let her have fun!

Dramatic play is a form of free play for your child to express herself. It is one of the most personal, individualistic, and intimate learning experiences your child can engage in because through dramatic play your child can explore the world by taking on the role of someone else or work through her feelings by recreating a familiar situation.

Overall, it is important to encourage your child to participate in dramatic play because it offers a wide range of opportunities for two year olds to use and expand their cognitive, language, literacy, memory, and social skills.

ACTIVITY

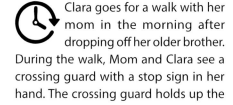

Clara goes for a walk with her mom in the morning after dropping off her older brother. During the walk, Mom and Clara see a crossing guard with a stop sign in her hand. The crossing guard holds up the stop sign, and together Mom and Clara cross the street safely.

When Clara gets home, Mom hears her yell "Stop!" She goes to Clara's room and notices that Clara has lined up all her dolls and is having them cross the road after she says "Stop!" to imaginary cars.

INSIGHT

Clara creates a play experience that is familiar to her and acts it out using her dolls and an imaginary stop sign and vehicles. This is an example of an everyday activity blossoming into a dramatic play opportunity.

5. Physical Development

> **Physical development in two year olds includes gross motor, fine motor, and sensory motor experiences.**

A motor skill is defined as a physical capability.

You have probably already noticed your child has become more coordinated in his gross motor (large muscle) movements. Not only has he developed a much smoother, heel-to-toe form of walking, but he is also able to maneuver around corners, walk backward, and avoid running into things.

In addition, your child is combining his senses to engage in more complex sensory motor skills like kicking a ball and walking up and down steps; however, even though your child is displaying more coordinated movements, it is important to remember that his judgment and self-control are still lagging when it comes to testing his physical limits, both indoors and outside.

Fine motor skills usually take more time to develop than gross motor skills as they require more hand-eye coordination and concentration. Your two year old is still building the attention skills he needs to develop fine motor skills such as tracing and writing.

This year you will see your child engaging in fine motor movements such as grasping, reaching, releasing, and turning his wrist. He will become interested in building with blocks, turning doorknobs, and turning the pages of a book.

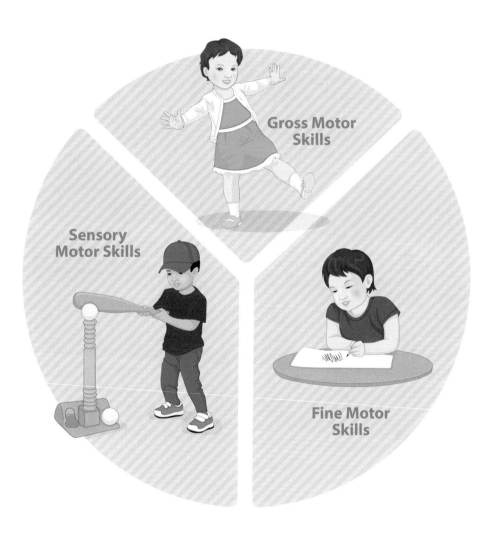

WHOLE CHILD: AGE TWO
Physical
Development Components

These fine motor movements will also play a part in your child building his independence through developing more self-help skills such as getting undressed and washing his hands.

Because fine motor skills take longer and are harder to develop, it is important to provide a wide variety of opportunities for two year olds to enhance their fine motor development.

So even though your child's physical growth has started to slow down this year compared to when he was an infant, you will see him continue to make tremendous strides in his physical development.

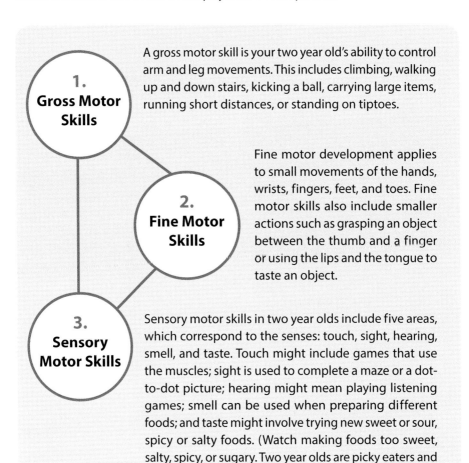

1. Gross Motor Skills

A gross motor skill is your two year old's ability to control arm and leg movements. This includes climbing, walking up and down stairs, kicking a ball, carrying large items, running short distances, or standing on tiptoes.

2. Fine Motor Skills

Fine motor development applies to small movements of the hands, wrists, fingers, feet, and toes. Fine motor skills also include smaller actions such as grasping an object between the thumb and a finger or using the lips and the tongue to taste an object.

3. Sensory Motor Skills

Sensory motor skills in two year olds include five areas, which correspond to the senses: touch, sight, hearing, smell, and taste. Touch might include games that use the muscles; sight is used to complete a maze or a dot-to-dot picture; hearing might mean playing listening games; smell can be used when preparing different foods; and taste might involve trying new sweet or sour, spicy or salty foods. (Watch making foods too sweet, salty, spicy, or sugary. Two year olds are picky eaters and will reject flavors that are too strong.)

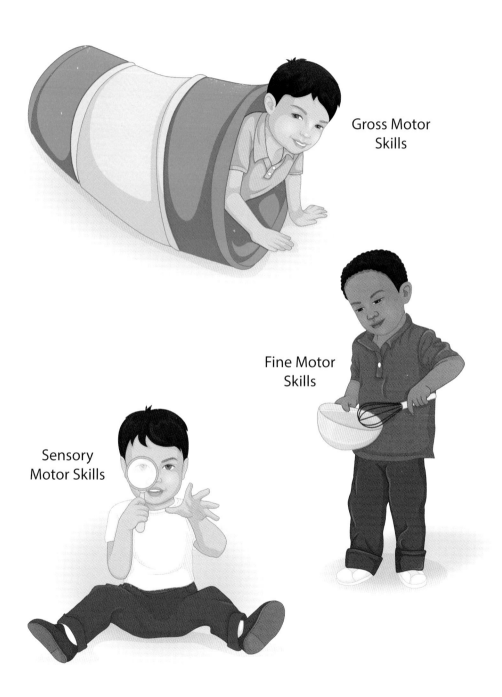

Gross Motor Skills

Fine Motor Skills

Sensory Motor Skills

Gross Motor Skills >
Large Muscles

Gross motor skills are the larger movements your child makes with her arms, legs, feet, or her entire body.

ACTIVITY

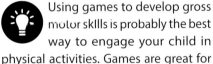 Mom and her daughter Morgan are getting ready to have lunch. Mom thinks it would be nice to play a game of Row, Row, Row Your Boat since they read the book earlier that day. Mom tells Morgan to sit so that they are facing each other, and they hold hands. They then begin to rock back and forth and sing the song "Row, Row, Row Your Boat." They start off slowly and then speed up, pretending that the boat has hit rocky seas.

INSIGHT

Using games to develop gross motor skills is probably the best way to engage your child in physical activities. Games are great for fun bonding, too.

Gross motor activities are movements of the entire body such as the ability to roll over, walk, hop, climb, crawl, and jump. These activities increase blood flow, which feeds the brain.

Movement experiences should be introduced early in life and built upon year after year with classes and team sports.

Guidelines for Everyday Gross Motor Activities

Your child should have at least 30 minutes of structured (adult-lead) physical activity each day. The following activities can be fun for the entire family: taking a walk in the neighborhood or playing T-ball. Activities such as T-ball also help to develop ball skills such as catching, throwing, kicking, and hitting.

Your child should engage in 60 minutes or more of unstructured (free play) physical activity each day and should not be inactive for more than 60 minutes at a time, except when sleeping. If your child is involved in active play at an early age she will stay active and be physically fit in the future.

A great example of unstructured play would be taking your child to the neighborhood park and using the playground equipment. Encourage your child to go on the slide; because she needs to climb up stairs and position her body to sit on the slide so that she does not tip over, she develops balance and strength.

As your child develops, her gross motor skills will go from mastery of simple skills like jumping and crawling to more complex skills like riding a tricycle and standing on one foot.

Fine Motor Skills >

Small Muscles

Fine motor skills refer to the small movements of the hands, wrists, fingers, feet, and toes.

Fine motor activities are built on four basic skills. These skills include releasing objects, grasping for objects, reaching for objects, and turning the wrist in various directions.

To support your child's fine motor skills you should make one of the following activities a part of your weekly activities at home:

* Mold and roll play dough into balls.
* Tear newspaper into strips.
* Squeeze water from a sponge.
* Roll small balls out of tissue paper.
* Sing songs with hand movements.
* Play clapping games.

Releasing

Releasing objects can be seen when your child is building with blocks. In order to build a tower, she has to pick up the block and then stack/release the block on top of another block. This is great for hand-eye coordination, as well as grasping and releasing movements.

Grasping scissors and then releasing them so she can cut paper is also a fine motor skill. Your child's mastery of grasping skills will not completely develop until she is three. Having your two year old pick up a bead (grasp) and place it on the string (release) helps strengthen fine motor muscles that your child will later need to build her writing skills.

Grasping

Grasping objects involves your two year old holding a writing instrument such as a pencil or crayon. Grasping objects can be seen in an activity such as scribbling.

ACTIVITY

 You are working in your home office. While you are writing something, your daughter is scribbling on a piece of paper with crayons. She is so excited to show you how she is "writing" just like you.

INSIGHT

Random scribbles come first, and then circular scribbles begin to emerge.

Reaching Objects

Your child's hand-eye coordination skills have improved as she has gotten older. This has lead to your child being able to have better small muscle control (grasping), which supports her ability to reach and grasp for objects because her hands and arms are working together to complete a task (picking up a ball and holding it or picking up a crayon from the table and grasping it).

Your child is now using her hand and arm together, and both arms are usually used together as well. You will see your two year old demonstrate a hand preference, if that one hand initiates the activity more often than the other. She moves her arm and hand together to get an object that she wants, and she usually starts by using the same arm and hand to reach for the object.

Hand preference is still emerging at this age, so it is not yet firmly established. As a result, your child may frequently reach for objects with alternating hands.

Turning the Wrist

This fine motor skill of turning the wrist involves your child moving his hand in circular motions. Working on this strengthens small muscles, which leads to further development of fine motor skills. Turning of the wrist movement is another fine motor skill that will lead to building strong writing skills as your child approaches age four.

ACTIVITY

Peter is in the kitchen with his mom watching him. She is watching him make a cake. Peter says, "I want to make a cake!" Mom gives Peter a plastic bowl and a small whisk so that he can "whip" ingredients like she does. Mom says, "Peter, watch how I turn the whisk around and around. Now you try." Peter starts turning his wrist just like Mom. "I did it!" he says.

INSIGHT

Activities that involve your child whisking or scooping will support the strengthening of your child's wrist and support the development of further fine motor skills.

Sensory Motor Skills >

Touchy Feely

Sensory motor experiences include activities that combine sight, touch, and hearing with fine and gross motor movements.

ACTIVITY

 Charlie and his father are at the park playing a game of T-ball, which involves hitting a ball off a stationary tee.

This is a good activity for Charlie to develop his sensory motor skills, because he has to see the ball while swinging the bat in order to make contact between the ball and the bat.

INSIGHT

 In the activity, Dad can point to the ball to direct Charlie about what to hit. Charlie would then know what to look at when it comes to swinging the bat and making contact with the ball. Practicing movements like these leads to mastery over time.

For your two year old to jump up and down on a square, he must see the square and use balance to land on the square. In order for your child to Velcro close his shoes, he must have adequate fine motor skills and be able to use the sense of touch to grab the Velcro and fasten it.

Your child is now seeing obstacles that might cause him to stumble ahead of time, whereas before he might just have tripped. He can now balance, jump, and walk and hold things at the same time. This is because he is now using his vision and attention skills to see what is in front of him and can adjust his movements and balance. Sensory motor skills heighten your child's reflexes and responses because the child is using a combination of senses to be more aware of his environment.

Your child also uses his hearing to follow two- and three-step requests that may involve large muscle movements ("Walk to the trash can and throw away the paper."). He will incorporate his listening and understanding skills to direct his attention to items being named and directions such as "stop" and "go."

Sensory motor skills bring together your child's cognitive skills through attention and reasoning when he uses his visual sense to make contact with items and move more gracefully throughout his environment. Sensory motor skills are part of his growing language skills as he understands and responds to directions. It is important to remember that sight, touch, and hearing must all work together to support development of your child's gross motor skills.

As your child matures, so do his senses and ability to use his senses to improve his motor skills.

Remember, the Whole Child Parenting Program offers appropriate developmental products and monthly activity books that walk you through supporting your child's skills. Using these in conjunction with the recommended age-appropriate room materials ensures faster development.

6. Health and Care

> Your two year old is more active than ever and is exploring everything around her.

She is also running, jumping, and working up a sweat! There are a number of tips and care routines you do to help your two year old stay clean, healthy, and happy from head to toe! When it comes to feeling under the weather, your two year old will start letting you know how she feels and point to what hurts. She may point to her tummy if she is constipated or pull on her ear if she has an ear infection. Other times, changes in your child can be an indication that she has a fever or is in pain. Irritability can affect not just her mood but also her schedule. It can also affect her sleeping or eating habits.

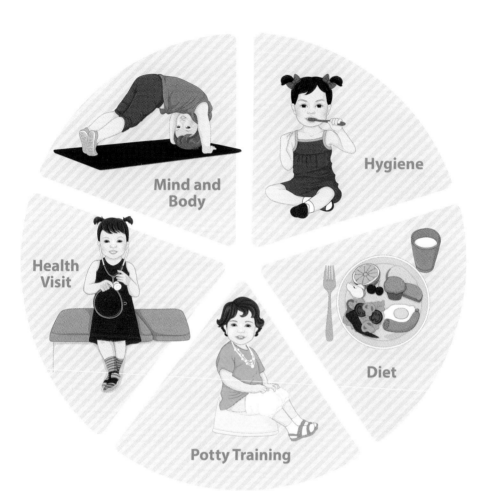

WHOLE CHILD: AGE TWO

Health and Care

Hygiene > Hair, Eyes, Ears, Skin, Nails, and Tooth Care

Working Together

* Let your child use the comb in her hair or on a doll before combing her hair yourself.

* When in the bath, let your child rub her fingers in the shampoo just like you do. You can let her wash her doll's hair in the tub as well.

* Let your child watch you wash her hair by placing a mirror next to the bathtub.

Hair Care

Your two year old's oil glands on her scalp and body don't become fully functional until puberty, so shampoo only as needed. Once a week is usually plenty.

Brushing

Brushing hair can help bring oils to the surface of the scalp. When trying to get out knots and tangles, try using a detangling spray and a wide-toothed comb or a brush with round-tipped bristles. Start combing or brushing out the ends and then work your way up to the scalp to avoid tugging and pulling.

Curly and Textured Hair

There are a number of products out there for curly and textured hair. **Try a variety of products to see which one fits your child best.** A good product for your child's hair is one that doesn't dry it out or weigh it down. With curly or textured hair, it is also a good idea to keep the hair short, let it air dry, and brush through it with just your hands or a wide-toothed comb only when wet to avoid frizz.

Eye Care

Your child's eyes can still change up to the age of two.

Check your child's eyes regularly to see if:

* your child's eyes are crossed,
* they are sensitive to light,
* one eye is wandering,
* both eyes cannot follow an object as it moves back and forth in front of her.

Conjunctivitis (Pink Eye)

Conjunctivitis has three forms: viral, bacterial, or allergic.

Symptoms usually include:
* watery discharge,
* veiny redness in the white area of an eye,
* itchy and swollen eyes,
* stringy discharge that causes eyelids to stick together, especially after sleeping.

Viral and bacterial conjunctivitis are contagious and usually occur from an upper respiratory tract infection, sore throat, or cold.

Conjunctivitis requires a doctor; you will need a prescription for antibiotic drops or ointments.

Allergic conjunctivitis is not contagious and is usually connected to seasonal allergies, irritation, or intolerance to medication or anything topical that is put on the face and comes in contact with your child's eyes. A cold compress can also relieve discomfort.

Ear Care

At bath time, clean the outside crevices of your child's ear with a damp, soft cloth.

DO NOT probe the inside of the ear. The middle ear is not fully developed, and you could end up puncturing the eardrum or pushing wax farther into your child's ear.

Ear Infections

Ear infections are most common in the middle ear. Until the age of three, the Eustachian tube that connects the outer and inner ear has not yet fully developed or grown. Because it is so small, the Eustachian tube gets clogged after a child has a cold.

Signs that your child has an ear infection may be pulling on her ear or seeing drainage come from her ear.

Skin Care

Dry skin can occur due to the weather as well as dehydration.

When caring for your child's skin:

* Try cutting back on bath time and sticking to 10-minute baths.
* Use a moisturizer on your two year old's body as soon as he gets out of the bath, before all the moisture in the skin evaporates.
* Have your two year old drink more fluids.
* Add more fatty foods to his diet such as avocados, flax seed, and olive oil.

When cleaning dry skin:

* Pat down skin and make sure not to wipe rough, chapped skin (especially face and cheeks).
* Use warm water (avoid hot water).
* Use an alcohol- and perfume-free moisturizer.
* Apply sunscreen when going outside because your child's sensitive skin can burn easily, causing his cheeks to be dry and predisposing him to skin cancer later in life.

Nail Care

Your two year old is constantly playing and exploring, so it is not uncommon for him to get play dough, food, or dirt in his fingernails. Try to keep your child's fingernails short so that they collect the least amount of dirt. **Wash your two year old's hands frequently, especially after activities or outside time.** You can use a nail brush or toothbrush to help clean under your two year old's fingernails.

Trimming

Trim your two year old's fingernails after getting out of the bath. The water softens the nails, making them easier to trim and cut. Sing a counting song or count the fingers to keep your child engaged and patient while you finish.

Tooth Care

Try to get your child in the habit of brushing her teeth as more teeth start to come in. Get a small-head toothbrush with soft, round bristles and brush your two year old's teeth gently in a circular motion along the sides and along the outer gum lines.

Brushing can help clean any food stuck in teeth and massage your two year old's gums while she is teething. Let her brush her own teeth for a little while before you take over.

Skip toothpaste until your child masters spitting out the toothpaste.

Teach your child to rinse by leaning over the sink and spitting. **Have your child say words like** *nuts* **or** *tooth* **to help her spit into the sink.**

Diet and your child's teeth:

Diet plays a key role in your child having healthy teeth. It is important to have her rinse her mouth out after eating or snacking. This is why brushing at night time is the most important!

Here are a few tips for snacking and mealtime:

* Snacks and meals should be served around the same time each day.

* Limit snacks in between meals. One reason is because you want your child to be hungry for mealtime. The other is because frequent snacking without brushing immediately afterward leads to plaque and tooth decay.

* When your child does snack include food that will help support healthy teeth. For example, raw broccoli, low-fat yogurt, or fruits like pear and melon cut into bite-size pieces.

* Remember to choose foods with low sugar content. Try to avoid processed foods whenever possible.

Diet >
Calories, Picky Eaters, Allergies, and Tummy Troubles

Two year olds need:

* 5 ounces of grains (one slice of bread or ½ cup of cooked rice or pasta),
* 1 ½ cups of fruits (¾ cups juice, ½ cup canned fruit, ¼ cup dried fruit, 1 piece of fruit or melon wedge),
* 1 ½ cups of vegetables (½ cup chopped raw or cooked vegetables, 1 cup raw leafy greens),
* 2 cups of milk or other dairy products,
* 2–4 ounces of high-protein foods (meat, poultry, eggs, and legumes)—1 ounce meat, 1 egg, ¼ cup legumes such as beans, 2 tablespoons of peanut butter,
* 3–4 teaspoons of healthy oils such as canola oil, olive oil, or tub margarine,
* Fats and sweets are empty calories and should be avoided.

Calories

Two-year old boys and girls need an average of 1,000 calories each day for healthy weight maintenance.

Based on the activity level of each child, two year olds may need more or less than the average. The more active the child, the more calories she will need.

* The food quantity averages to the left refer to two year olds who engage in 30–60 minutes of physical activity per day.

Calculate how many calories your two year old needs.

The average child needs 34–41 calories per pound of body weight each day.

Picky Eaters?

Offer your opinionated two year old two healthful options so she feels like she is more in control. Put small portions on her plate at first so she does not feel overwhelmed and then add more food after she finishes the first serving.

Adding dipping sauces or encouraging your two year old to be a part of making the meal can make her more excited about eating (let her assemble the sandwich or spread peanut butter and place raisins on celery for ants on a log).

Two year olds are becoming more social, so sit down for lunch or other mealtimes with your child. Moving from a highchair to a booster seat encourages more socializing. In addition, by sitting your child closer to you at the table, you can model how to use utensils and how to act at the table.

Utensils

Two year olds should be moving toward using utensils such as a spoon and cup. Nonskid plates and bowls help your two year old scoop food into her spoon. Cut up her foods into small, bite-size pieces so that she can easily go from spoon or fork to mouth.

Allergies

With the introduction of more varieties of food, some two year olds begin to develop allergies. Indications of allergies include sneezing, itching, swelling, and skin rashes.

Food allergies are usually quite rare and follow family genetics. If you have a food allergy that runs in your family, be careful when giving your child that food.

Food allergies in young children can go away with age.

Hay fever can occur with environmental or seasonal allergies when your child is allergic to pollen, grass, dust, or animal dander. Symptoms include watery eyes, sneezing, and a runny nose.

Because two year olds cannot yet blow their noses to clear their nasal passages, mucus drips down their throats, causing them to cough.

Tummy Troubles

Your two year old's digestive system is starting to change because your child is having more consistent bowel movements, and new textures of foods are being introduced. Your child may complain about stomach pain if he has to go to the bathroom and isn't yet in control of the feeling or is feeling emotionally stressed and can't put together the words to tell you. **Most complaints about stomachaches with two year olds are minor and can be helped by giving your child something to eat or having him try to go potty.** If his stomach pain is accompanied by a fever or vomiting, he may be sick.

Constipation

Constipation is not always a sign of illness but can make your child uncomfortable. Constipation is usually accompanied by hard or painful stools.

What to do:

* Increase fluid intake: Give your child more water to drink.
* Diet: Make sure you are giving your child correct portion sizes when it comes to food, and also change the variety of foods you serve. Provide more fruits and vegetables.
* Try prunes, dried fruits (raisins and apricots), oatmeal, or green vegetables.
* Stay away from cow's milk, yogurt, cheese, cooked carrots, and bananas when constipated.

Diarrhea

Diarrhea is the opposite of constipation and involves very loose or too many bowel movements. Diarrhea can cause your child pain as well as make him become dehydrated and lethargic. Diarrhea can be caused by a virus or contaminated food or can be a side effect of medication.

If diarrhea starts quickly but ends by the next meal your child eats and isn't accompanied by fever, you probably should not be concerned.

What to do:

* Try bananas, white toast, white rice, and electrolytes to drink (such as Pedialyte®).
* Avoid drinks with sugar like soda or ginger ale because the sugar in the drinks may upset your child's stomach.

If his stomach pain is accompanied by a fever or vomiting, he may be sick.

Vomiting

Vomiting is usually the result of a virus caused by bacteria or a parasite. It can sometimes be followed by diarrhea.

Vomiting can also cause dehydration. Signs of dehydration include:

* not urinating,
* dry lips and mouth,
* looking pale.

What to do:

If your child is having trouble holding down liquids or food, try to rehydrate him with an oral rehydration solution.

Examples of oral rehydration solutions include:

* water,
* Pedialyte®,
* watered-down juice,
* chicken broth.

When administering oral rehydration solutions:

1. Give your child only a teaspoon of fluid every five minutes to help him keep it down.

2. If your child is able to keep down the liquid, keep increasing the amount of fluid you give him.

3. Keep giving your child fluids until he stops vomiting.

4. If your child is ready to eat again, try to stick to these foods:

* dry toast,
* small amount of pasta (no sauce),
* hard-boiled egg,
* rice,
* bananas.

Potty Training >
Are We Ready?

Eighteen months to three years old is the average age to show interest in and start trying to potty train.
Your child may be ready to begin potty training if your child:

* begins to communicate having a dirty diaper—your child may verbally tell you or draw your attention to his diaper by patting it or pointing to it;

* begins to show discomfort when wet or soiled—walking in a wide stride or beginning to pull and take off his soiled diaper;

* shows interest in the potty—models potty training with toys, dolls, or even themselves;

* demonstrates independence—starting to pull his pants on and off, follows basic one- and two-step directions;

* is able to stay dry for up to two hours between diaper changes—shows that the bladder is maturing and is able to hold it in longer;

* starts to have regular bowel movements at the same time every day.

Ready to Start?

* Stay close to home.

* Try no underpants or underwear.

* Try to encourage the most tries as possible so your child can get used to the feeling of going.

* Use a timer to teach the feeling of going regularly.

* Give your child salty snacks to make him thirsty or let him have a special juice he likes.

* Have all materials present at the potty (toilet paper, underwear or pullup, clean clothing).

* Let him bring his favorite toy, doll, or stuffed animal to model potty training.

Follow Through

Potty on the go

Invest in a travel potty to encourage consistency. It is important to keep up with your routine even when at Grandma's house, with your baby-sitter, or at school.

* The more days you get into potty training, the more consistent your child's potty times will become. Having a routine with nap and eating times adds to the consistency. **Routine allows you to be able to know times to encourage your child to try if she has not expressed to you herself that she has to go.**

* Have all your materials with you, such as wipes, clean underwear, and plastic bags for soiled clothes.

Potty time doesn't mean missing play time!

Don't make your child feel like going potty means she is missing out on an activity or other interesting or exciting things going on.

* Move the potty to the activity. If everyone is outside, let your child use the potty while she is outside so she doesn't put up a fight to leave because she feels like she is missing out.

* Encourage your child to try before you start an activity or before you go somewhere. Have your child try before lunch and after lunch, as well as before you start a game or put out different toys.

Potty training tips for help along the journey:

* Every 15 minutes, put your child on the potty, then put back on the diaper or pullups for three days. On the third day, have an all-day no diaper or pullup session.

* Have naked time; let your child wear nothing so that your child has to put the pee and poop somewhere.

* Give rewards such as stickers for the first full day in underwear.

* Make sure you read (see to the right) the differences in potty training boys and girls.

* Be proactive when you go out or drop your child at a neighbor's house. Bring a portable potty chair with you and encourage your child to ask to use it when she needs to.

Things That Come With Time . . .

Pooping on the potty usually takes children a little longer to master because it involves having to push out their poop, and that can take some getting used to and definitely requires a longer time sitting on the potty.

When you start to see a pattern as to what time of the day your child has a bowel movement, try to plan your schedule around that time so that she is more encouraged to try on a regular basis. For example, if your child usually poops about half an hour after lunch, plan a short activity or extend cleanup time and then have her sit down and try. That way, she won't get too busy with another activity and try to speed through potty time.

Encourage your child to keep trying. Charts with stickers are a great way for your child to be proud of all the times she sat on the potty.

Boys vs. Girls

Have girls sit farther back on the potty with their knees apart. This will relax their muscles as well as make them more comfortable if they end up sitting and trying for a few extra minutes. Adding a stepstool for her when she gets older and is sitting on the toilet can help her relax, too.

Boys will start using the potty while sitting down so that they can focus more on the feeling of having to urinate and take the pressure off learning to aim. When they are ready to urinate standing up, it may be a good idea to get a stepstool for your toilet to make it easier on him.

Finding something flushable for boys to aim at will help. Gummy bears or mints work great and can be an incentive as well. If he aims at the gummy bear in the toilet, then he can have a fresh one to eat when he is done.

Remember: Every child is different. Do not force your child into potty training. If your child doesn't show an interest right away or puts up a fight, try again in a couple of months.

Health Visit >
What to Expect During a Wellness Visit

The well-child visits during your child's second year are similar to those you had when she was younger, though now you can expect to have deeper discussions with your doctor about behavior and habits.

Fevers

Once your child is two, you can take your child's temperature via the axillary method (underarm) or orally (mouth). To help your child keep a thermometer in long enough to get an accurate temperature, try holding a timer your child can watch or hold a thermometer under your armpit or in your mouth at the same time.

Underarm:
96° F to 99° F is a normal temperature; 99.6° F and up means a fever is present.

Mouth:
96° F to 99° F is a normal temperature; 99.4° F and up means a fever is present.

Eighty to ninety percent of all fevers in young children are related to self-limiting infections (these infections get better without treatment).

Unless a fever rises above 102° F, try these methods of treatment:

* Increase fluids: Fevers can occur if your child is dehydrated.

* Cool down: You don't want to overheat your child, so cool her down by having her wear fewer layers and bring in a fan. Make sure your child is comfortable and not too cold.

* Slow down: Discourage running around or heavy activity that can increase temperature.

Common Cold

Colds are also known as upper respiratory disorders and are usually caused by rhinoviruses, which spread from hand to hand. The duration of a cold is usually seven to ten days, although some symptoms, such as a cough or runny nose, can linger longer.

The average child gets six to eight colds per year.

Symptoms of a cold:

* runny nose
* nasal congestion
* sneezing
* dry cough
* fatigue
* crankiness
* loss of appetite
* a mild fever
* sore, scratchy throat

Treatments for a cold:

* plenty of warm fluids and vitamin C-enriched foods,
* humidifiers to help clear nasal passages,
* saline solutions to soften dry mucus that clogs your child's nostrils.

To help prevent a cold: wash hands, disinfect toys, and clean surfaces on a regular basis to get rid of germs.

Your child's checkup will include:

* a complete physical examination;
* measurement of your child's length, weight, and head circumference; growth will be plotted on a growth chart;
* a review of your two year old's development through simple observation. How is she walking: on tiptoes or flat feet? Is she combining two words? The doctor may ask you these questions and others like them;
* safety questions such as asking if your child is in an age-appropriate car seat;
* a discussion of your child's eating habits. Is she eating a variety of foods? Using a spoon? Using a cup? Weaned from the pacifier?;
* advice on what to expect in the coming year;
* immunizations;
* discussion between you and the doctor. Talk about any questions or concerns you have, and write down any specific instructions the doctor gives you regarding special care. Keep updating your child's permanent medical record, listing information on growth and any problems or illnesses.

Immunizations

Most doctors schedule your child's two-year-old visit on your child's actual two-year-old birthday. Your doctor will weigh and measure your child as well as ask you questions about your child's development and overall health.

Your doctor will discuss your child's eating habits as well as examine your child's teeth for tooth decay, abnormal tooth development, or other problems and recommend visiting a dentist no later than your child's third birthday.

The two-year-old checkup includes a number of screenings and required immunizations.

You child will be screened for anemia, lead poisoning, tuberculosis, and high cholesterol.

Lastly, your doctor will talk to you about other safety issues such as wearing helmets when riding bikes or scooters or skating and how to stay germ free.

The immunization chart on the next page can give you an idea of the ones required early in life.

Well-child visits with a pediatrician are yearly routines that will continue through the adolescent years.

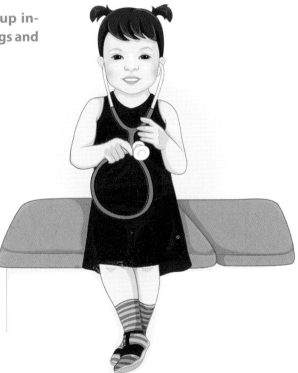

Recommended immunizations by age two:

Age	Birth	2 months	4 months	6 months	12–18 months	19–24 months
HepB Hepatitis B	✔	✔	✔	✔		
DTap Diphtheria, Tetanus, Pertussiss		✔	✔	✔	✔	✔
HiB Haemophilius Influenzae Type B		✔	✔	✔	✔	
Polio		✔	✔	✔		
PCV Pneumo-coccal Conjugate		✔	✔	✔	✔	
RV Rotavirus		✔	✔	✔		
MMR Measles, Mumps, Rubella					✔	✔
VAR Varicella					✔	✔
HepA Hepatitus A					✔	
HPV Human Pappiloma-virus						
MCV4 Meningo-coccal Conjugate						
In Influenza				✔		✔

Mind and Body >
Yoga

Having two year olds participate in yoga gives them the ability to exercise both their bodies and minds.

Yoga encompasses the whole child by strengthening bodies and calming minds to encourage better focus and build self-confidence. Through yoga, children are able to develop and foster more than just physical skills. Yoga helps your two year old develop social-emotional skills such as self-awareness.

Physically, your two year old is developing more body awareness through yoga by testing and pushing her balancing and physical capabilities. She is able to become more confident and have higher self-esteem when it comes to movement and mobility.

Yoga is a great tool to build creativity and imagination. Your child can express herself through different movements. As a parent, you can incorporate different music, relatable animal or nature poses, and dance. Because your child is young, you will have to show her how to do each movement.

1. Three-Legged Dog Pose

Step both feet together so your big toes are touching. Bend over and put your hands flat on the floor in front of you. Shift your weight onto your hands and your left foot, then raise your right leg into the air. Then lower your right leg and switch sides.

2. Frog Pose

Bend your knees and sit down. Place your palms on the ground, but make sure your knees don't touch. Move your heels upward and put a little pressure on your toes. Slowly, put your heels on the floor and stand up.

3. Reverse Warrior Pose

With the right knee bent, drop left hand down to rest on left leg. Then reach right arm up toward the ceiling on an inhale. Keep right knee bent and press firmly into feet, keeping legs strong. When you feel solid, begin sinking hips down. Check to make sure shoulders are soft. Hold the pose for up to five breaths, and repeat it on the other side.

1. Three-Legged Dog Pose

2. Frog Pose

3. Reverse Warrior Pose

Remember, the Whole Child Parenting Program offers appropriate developmental products and monthly activity books that walk you through supporting your child's skills. Using these in conjunction with the recommended age-appropriate room materials ensures faster development.

Reaching Milestones >

Your child is two years old, now ranging in age from 24–36 months. At this age your child will develop very quickly and will develop most of these skills as he approaches the age of three. Now, as a two year old, his learning process has become more thoughtful. He's beginning to form mental images for objects, actions, and concepts. He also can solve some problems in his head, performing mental trial and error.

Now is a great time to get in the habit of checking your child's progress on a more frequent basis. You can do this twice a year or every three months. Time passes quickly and you can miss progress in the blink of an eye.

The information below is a guide to explain some of the developmental milestones an average two year old will achieve. Theses skills may not all occur in order; skills can occur within a six-month to a year range. Consider what you read in the context of your child's unique development.

COGNITIVE

- Places large puzzle pieces in appropriate empty spaces.
- Can sort shapes, complete puzzles with eight pieces or less, and stack a set of rings on a peg by size.
- Will begin to recognize the purpose of numbers in counting objects—especially the number two.
- Can solve simple problems with the "trial and error" method and will practice an activity many times to master it. Becomes much more interested in winding up toys and turning lights and appliances on and off.
- Recognizes patterns with daily activities and understands concepts like "tomorrow" and "yesterday."
- Spends about two minutes on a single activity. The usual preference is for almost constant attention from an adult. With or near a small group of children, can play peacefully for 10 minutes.

SOCIAL-EMOTIONAL

- Enjoys playing alongside other children, usually will keep to himself.
- He is more independent and can do things for himself (e.g. pour milk, dress himself in simple clothes).
- Begins to label feelings that he recognizes in himself and others. Controlling emotion is difficult, so frustrations may trigger emotional meltdowns.
- New fears—the dark, monsters, and people in costumes—will emerge. He does not really know the difference between fantasy and reality. Comfort objects like blankets or a teddy bear will be desired.
- Conflicts will require adults to step in to prevent aggression.

LANGUAGE

- Enjoys having books read to him and will pretend to "read" as he independently looks through familiar books.

- New language discoveries will lead to him picking up most parts of speech to form more complete sentences. Can understand and say hundreds of words.

- Makes a variety of scribble marks anywhere and everywhere and may attempt to write the first letter in his name in this scribble pattern.

- Sings A-B-C song.

- Understands simple directions and many common phrases used in routine situations.

CREATIVE

- Can make sounds by banging and shaking instruments and household items.

- Might substitute one object for another in play, like using Legos® to represent food in a mealtime scene. Acts out chants and simple songs.

- Draws a face (no arms and legs). Enjoys sensory pleasures of the art materials you provide and focuses on the process of creating art.

- Gains more control over his voice and joins in singing the refrains of favorite songs.

PHYSICAL

- May be able to ride a tricycle forward using the pedals and steer it around corners.

- Can kick a small ball forward, catch a rolled ball, and throw a ball overhand (with little accuracy).

- Can stand on one foot for a few seconds. Has learned to go up and down the stairs with only one foot on each step. Stands on tiptoes.

- Carries large toys or several toys while walking.

- Turns doorknobs, unscrews lids, and has improved his skills in using utensils.

HEALTH AND CARE

- Points to body parts.

- Helps with undressing and dressing, puts feet in shoes and arms in sleeves.

- Learns to use toilet.

- Feeds self with spoon.

Environment >
Two Year Old's Room

"Help me do it by myself" is probably the most important concept to keep in mind for your two year old.

It is important to intentionally create an environment that will help her learn and gain as much independence as possible. There's no better place to do this than in your home.

Your home is already a rich environment full of learning opportunities. We will help you set up practical activities that will tap into her natural curiosity and support her ability to test the world around her.

This can best be achieved by designing a space with materials and toys that stimulate thinking, creativity, and support all **six areas of development (cognitive, language, social emotional, creative, physical, and health).**

The goal is for your child to have an area in her room that is well organized using your **Six Drawer Whole Child Color-Coded Organizer.**

You are creating a space that's free from clutter, multi-functional, and efficient. At right is a sample of a two year old's room with must-have items for optimal learning.

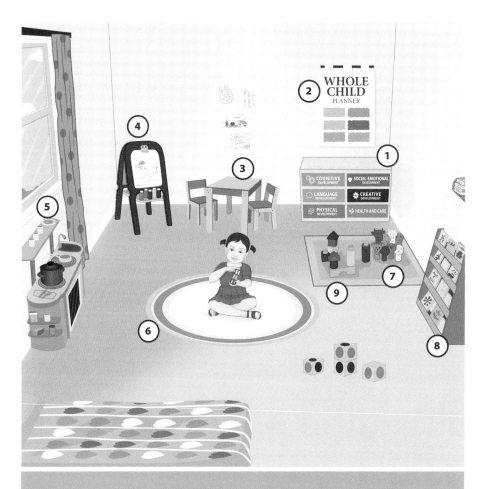

Whole Child: Two Year Old's Room

The following list contains must-have items for your two year old's room. These items will be used interchangeably with your other Whole Child Parenting materials.

1. Six Drawer Whole Child Color-Coded Organizer
2. Whole Child Wall Planner
3. Table and Chairs
4. Easel
5. Kitchen Set
6. Carpet
7. Puppet/Pretend Play Materials
8. Bookshelf
9. Blocks and Manipulatives

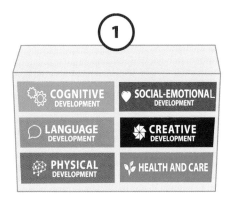

1. Six Drawer Whole Child Color-Coded Organizer

Easily organize educational materials and toys by six areas of development. Ensure your child always has enough materials in each drawer.

2. Whole Child Wall Planner

Plan and organize weekly activities based on six areas of development.

3. Table and Chairs

Provides a clearly defined space, at child's level and shaped to support posture, for child to work independently and stay focused. Use for fine motor development and learning shapes, colors, spatial concepts, science, letters, and numbers.

4. Easel

Provides a place for child to play with well-organized art materials displayed at eye level. Materials are easily changed out by child with help or by parent. Use for fostering development of child's aesthetic sense and for engaging in creative experiences.

5. Kitchen Set

Organize props and pretend food.
Can be easily rotated in and out.
Use to develop self-help skills,
independence, and imagination.

6. Carpet

Provides a soft, safe place, free
from clutter, for your child to play
on. Use for providing materials in
one central location at child's eye
level. Enables parent to change out
materials and still maintain child
safety.

7. Puppet/Pretend Play Materials

Helps social communication, and
interactive skills through shared
experiences. Use for pretend play
and peek-a-boo games.

8. Bookshelf

Makes books easily
accessible to child and
supports independent
exploration and literacy skills.
Use for bonding with child
through one-on-one time.

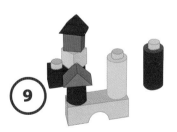

9. Blocks and Manipulatives

Use for construction and spatial
skill development while talking
about shapes, sizes, colors. Helps
develop recognition, counting,
sorting, and matching skills.

whole child activity books >

Have a look at a sample of our series of activity books for two year olds. This series of 12 titles helps two year olds exercise their brains and bodies in every category of development explored in the Whole Child Parenting books. The 12 titles are available now.

WHOLE CHILD

Age 2

Activity Book

P

Transportation

WHOLE CHILD = $\dfrac{\text{smart} + \text{creative}}{\text{healthy} + \text{happy}}$

COGNITIVE
DEVELOPMENT

Problem-solving · Attention · Numbers

SOCIAL-EMOTIONAL
DEVELOPMENT

Self-control · Friendship · Feelings

LANGUAGE
DEVELOPMENT

Communication · Speaking · Literacy

CREATIVE
DEVELOPMENT

Dramatic Play · Dance · Music · Arts

PHYSICAL
DEVELOPMENT

Motor Skills: Sensory, Gross, Fine

HEALTH AND CARE

Hygiene · Diet · Routine · Yoga

sneak peek >

1

EARLY MATH SKILLS

DISCOVER!

At two years old your child is learning to identify and name numbers one through five and count in order up to three. She will begin to count and assign numbers to objects beyond three, but is still learning to do this in the correct order. She can also notice differences and similarities in shapes.

DID YOU KNOW?

Activities such as counting buttons on a shirt or pointing out shapes in your child's food foster the development of mathematical skills.

LET'S DO MORE!

Reinforce simple quantity concepts. Help your child understand the math words one and two. Give simple directions, such as asking her to "take one" or "pick two" of something.

CIRCLE

Skill • Recognizing shapes

Directions: Point to the circular wheels on the car and say "circle." Have her repeat the word *circle* after you. Have her color in the circles using a green crayon.

 Having your child color shapes that are the same size and orientation helps her focus on identifying shapes based upon their characteristics (size and shape).

27

sneak peek >

NUMBER TWO

Skill • Tracing numbers

Directions: Point to the number 2. Say "two" and have your child repeat after you. Count the number of buses together: "One, two." First have her trace the number 2 with her pointer finger (starting at the green dot and ending at the red dot). Next have her trace the number 2 using a green crayon.

 Number sense is seeing how numbers represent an amount. For example, how the symbol "2" is related to the quantity of two items.

MORE OR LESS

Skill • Learning spatial concepts

Directions: Have your child point to the road with *more* cars. Next have her point to the road with *fewer* cars. Have your child draw a circle around the road with *more* cars using a green crayon.

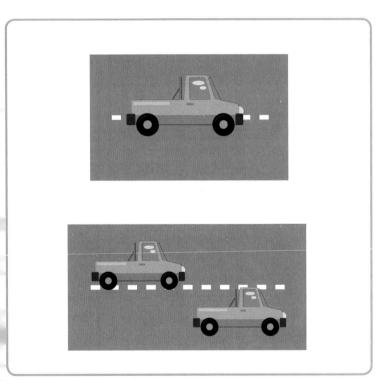

Learning the concepts of more and less leads to learning how to compare groups of objects based on their quantity.

sneak peek >

COGNITIVE
DEVELOPMENT

SOCIAL-EMOTIONAL
DEVELOPMENT

LANGUAGE
DEVELOPME

3

EARLY LANGUAGE SKILLS

DISCOVER!

Two year olds are noticing printed words all around them, from picture books to store signs. Exposing your child to printed words helps her begin to understand that words are made up of letters and that there is a connection between written words and letter sounds.

DID YOU KNOW?

By tracing the letter P with a crayon, you are giving your child fine motor skills practice that will later help her with learning to write.

LET'S DO MORE!

Point out print as it is found all around you. Show and read the words on exit signs, food labels, and storybooks to your child as part of your daily routine.

TOP TO BOTTOM

Skill • Tracing Lines

Directions: Look at the plane. Have your child trace the lines from *top* to *bottom* with her pointer finger (starting at the green dot and stopping at the red dot). Then have her trace the lines with a crayon.

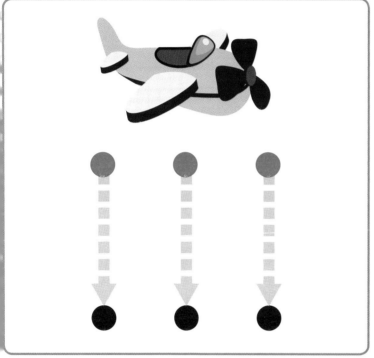

Tracing straight lines enables your child to create letters that are made up of straight lines.

53

sneak peek >

 **CREATIVE**
DEVELOPMENT

COLORING

Skill • Developing creativity

Directions: Give your child a blue and green crayon. Have him color the plane below, praising him for using both green and blue, regardless of the end result.

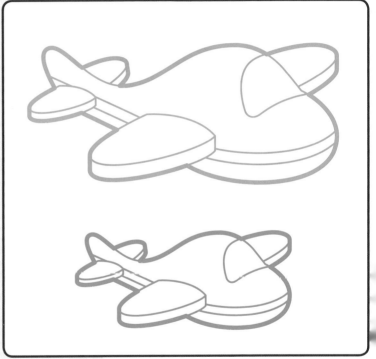

Being creative with colors enables your child to make connections between one area of learning (art) and another (color recognition).

CREATIVE
DEVELOPMENT

"I'M A LITTLE PLANE"

Skill • Rhyming

Directions: Read the rhyme below to your child. Give him crayons of different colors. Have him color the plane.

I'm a little plane.
(Raise arms at sides to shoulder height.)
Now watch me fly!
(Spin arms in front like a propeller.)

Here are my instruments
from down low to up high.
(With arms, reach from the ground to above the head.)

Making rhymes part of your daily routine will help your child memorize the words of his favorite songs and ditties.

59

sneak peek >

whole child parenting program >

Get a sneak peek into the next Whole Child Parenting book. ***Whole Child Parenting: Age Three*** is a comprehensive look into your three year old's development. The book is available now.

WHOLE CHILD
PARENTING

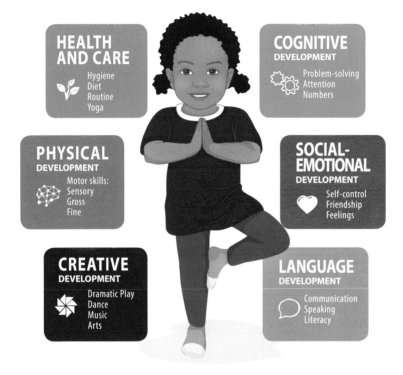

HEALTH AND CARE
Hygiene
Diet
Routine
Yoga

COGNITIVE DEVELOPMENT
Problem-solving
Attention
Numbers

PHYSICAL DEVELOPMENT
Motor skills:
Sensory
Gross
Fine

SOCIAL-EMOTIONAL DEVELOPMENT
Self-control
Friendship
Feelings

CREATIVE DEVELOPMENT
Dramatic Play
Dance
Music
Arts

LANGUAGE DEVELOPMENT
Communication
Speaking
Literacy

AGE THREE

Parents, educators, and caregivers
will learn how best to encourage growth and
skill-building in all six developmental areas.

sneak peek >

Milestones for a Three Year Old

COGNITIVE 1

- Names some colors
- Understands the concept of counting
- Recognizes some numbers and letters
- Develops a sense of time

SOCIAL-EMOTIONAL 2

- Acts more independent
- Plays with other children
- Develops empathy for others

LANGUAGE 3

- Speaks in five- to six-word sentences
- Tells stories
- Asks questions

CREATIVE 4

- Draws a person with two to four body parts
- Engages in pretend play with peers

PHYSICAL 5

- Moves forward and backward
- Stands on one foot for five seconds
- Kicks ball forward
- Copies and traces shapes

HEALTH AND CARE 6

- Gains independence with brushing teeth
- Develops daily routines
- Exhibits preschool readiness

three

At three years old, children have better control of their emotions and begin problem solving and thinking of solutions to their problems instead of acting out by hitting or screaming. They are developing a better sense of time and a clearer understanding of their daily routine. Because of this, three year olds are able to become more independent with personal care routines such as dressing and undressing themselves and washing their own hands. Three is a big year.

sneak peek >

1. Cognitive Development

> **Cognitive development skills enable your child to process information, reason through problems, and develop language and memory.**

Cognitive development is the building of thinking methods, which includes how your child will remember, problem solve, and make decisions from now and into adulthood.

Three year olds are able to sit and focus for longer periods of time, which enables them to take in more information. They also ask a lot of questions and are very inquisitive.

During cognitive development, children will grasp language, persevere through problems (like puzzles), ask a lot of questions (about things they see or hear), and remember past and upcoming events.

Remember, your child will develop at his own pace; however, there are still typical cognitive goals he must achieve during this age in order to be developing on track.

The following chart provides you with an image that walks you through the stages of your child's intellectual development.

Understanding these areas of cognitive development will help you learn how your child thinks, how to support learning, and how to teach new skills.

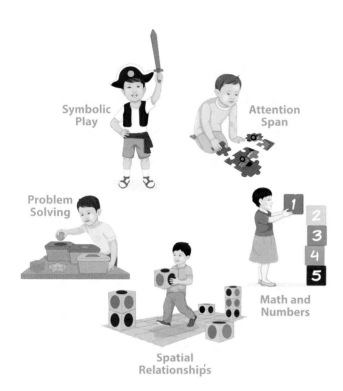

Symbolic Play

Attention Span

Problem Solving

Math and Numbers

Spatial Relationships

WHOLE CHILD: AGE THREE
Cognitive
Development Components

sneak peek >

Attention Span >
Stimulate My Brain

Attention span refers to the amount of time your child is able to concentrate on or focus on a single activity.

Supporting the development of your child's attention skills, along with his self-regulation skills, will form his foundation for learning. Strong attention skills will set the stage for your child to have success in everything from learning math to his social relationships. In addition, strong attention skills can help your child learn to read before age five, have improved memory, and achieve a host of other amazing milestones.

ACTIVITY

 Gabe wants to have a friend over for a play date. Mom agrees to have one friend come over. Mom says to Gabe, "Your friend is coming over. What should we do?" Gabe says, "A dance party! We love to dance. Look at me move." Mom thinks for a moment and says, "Okay! Dance party it is. You have to help me get things ready." Gabe says, "I'll get the music!" Gabe goes to his parents' room and grabs Mom's guitar for her. "Here you go, Mom!"

Gabe's friend arrives with her mom, and they go downstairs to have fun. In the beginning the children are talking and playing. Gabe's mom says, "It's time for a dance party!" Gabe and his friend scream "Yeah!" and jump up and down.

Mom tells the children, "For the first part of our dance party you can dance until the music stops. When the music stops you should stop dancing." Mom begins to play her guitar. After a few short minutes she stops and starts it again. After doing this several times, Gabe's mom says, "Now I want you to listen for me to strum the guitar fast. When you hear me stop you should stop dancing and listen." Gabe and his friend dance and stop for 30 seconds then dance again until they are all danced out. Gabe's friend says, "That was so fun, Gabe! Can I come to your house again?"

INSIGHT

Through this activity Mom gives the children an opportunity to practice attention skills, especially when she asks them to listen for the guitar playing. Mom also helps the children develop attention skills because this activity allows both children to actively participate as opposed to passively listen during the entire activity.

sneak peek >

Help build attention span

1. Speak a language of attention—Attention is a set of three skills: focus, awareness, and a set of mental skills that helps your child get things done, e.g. planning and decision making. Play Spot the Letter on a car ride. As you drive, call out a letter for your child to spot along the way, choosing easy to see objects like a stop sign for the letter S.

2. Focus on one another—A meeting of the minds comes from focusing on something together. Set the table for dinner together with your child.

3. White space, also known as uninterrupted time—Put an end to distractions to support developing attention skills in your child and provide a space for him to focus. Limit TV time, video games, and other electronics.

4. Eat mindfully—You may have noticed we are a society that eats on the run. Take time to stop and eat as a family, talking together about the food you are eating, how it smells, looks, and tastes.

Typically, your child will have the most difficulty with paying attention during activities that involve sitting and listening. This is normal behavior, and it occurs because at this age your child will become bored very easily and needs a variety of activities to stimulate his whole brain.

Your child's left side of the brain, which deals directly with logic, language, critical thinking, numbers, and reasoning can be referred to as the "seat of learning;" it is eager to take on new information. Provide lots of simple brain-stimulating activities so that your child can learn and develop his attention span.

Your three year old has a limited attention span. Build up attention skills over time. Do an activity for a minute, and then later do the same activity for a few minutes longer.

Over the next week, do at least two of the listed activities in the box to the left with your child. Start doing the activity every three days and then build up to every day. Building your child's attention span takes time and encouragement, and development must continue well into adolescence.

The quantity, quality, and consistency of stimulation you provide through experiences with your child will play a part in the developing structure of his brain and its capacity. By strengthening your child's brain, you will improve his ability to focus and pay attention to any task that he becomes involved in.

Remember, the Whole Child Parenting Program offers appropriate developmental products and monthly activity books that walk you through supporting your child's skills. Using these in conjunction with the recommended age-appropriate room materials ensures faster development.

sneak peek >

Math and Numbers >

I Spy with My Eyes

Math and number awareness involves your child counting, recognizing numbers and patterns, learning one-to-one correspondence, sorting, and classifying.

ACTIVITY

Adam is on the floor of his bedroom playing with a variety of toys he has taken out of his toy box. He discovers a few rocks of different sizes, a plastic frog, and a plastic tree branch.

Mom comes in his bedroom and says, "Adam, you're so quiet. What do you have?" He replies, "Look at all this stuff I found in my toy chest!" Mom replies, "Oh, wow! Look at this rock. It has all of these light colored lines on it." "Let me see," says Adam.

Mom asks, "Why don't we see how many other rocks we can find that look just like this rock here and count them?"

INSIGHT

Adam's experience playing with a collection of rocks is a powerful math experience. As he learns to match the rocks he is learning concepts of math through play and hands on experience. Mom supports her son by asking him to pay attention, notice how the rocks are the same, and group them in like categories. Mom also extends the learning experience by the two of them counting out how many rocks they have that look the same. Using simple materials and bonding together creates a meaningful math experience.

Mathematical thinking involves seeing how your child uses his brain to play with the concepts of parts and wholes and his ability to see math in everyday life.

Mathematical thinking is important for three reasons: it is a necessary skill to master in your child's schooling experience; it is a way of learning mathematics itself; and it helps your child in solving problems later in life.

One of the best ways to build early mathematical thinking skills in your child is to make numbers and math concepts fun and relatable to the everyday experiences he has. This will increase his desire to learn more and have an appreciation for math in the future.

Early math concepts appropriate for your child include shape sorting, matching games (putting one part with another part), color sorting, and simply playing with collections of things (seeing math in everyday life).

In this next example, you get a glimpse of how Maria is on her way to becoming a mathematician by interacting with ants. Learning about numbers is one of the first steps to your child becoming a mathematical thinker. She will become a mathematician through counting, number recognition, and one-to-one correspondence activities.

ACTIVITY

Maria is in her backyard kicking around a new ball Mom just bought her, when she accidentally kicks the ball in the area of the garbage cans. Maria runs over to get the ball and stops in her tracks, staring down at the ground. There are a bunch of ants in a line.

Maria runs inside to tell her dad. "Dad, come see the ants!" Maria grabs Dad's hand and heads toward the backyard. While she is walking with her dad, she begins to sing. "The ants go marching one by one, hurrah, hurrah. The ants go marching two by two, hurrah, hurrah."

Maria bends down to look at the ants on the ground and pulls Dad down with her. She tries to count the ants but they are just too small and numerous to count.

INSIGHT

Even though Maria cannot point to and count each ant on the ground, she is singing about numbers and uses simple counting while she sings the song and marches. This is counting using a **math rhyme**. It is simple and fun and happens through an everyday experience. You see how fun math can be for your child, and you have the distinct pleasure of being a part of the process!

Whole Child Parenting: Age Three
Available now >

WHOLE CHILD

Parenting Program books and materials are available worldwide.

The book that kick started the program!

Also available separately

Whole Child Program Activity Books

- 4 **Infant** Titles
- 6 **Toddler** Titles
- 12 **Age Two** Titles
- 12 **Age Three** Titles
- 12 **Age Four** Titles

Whole Child Program books and materials are available at special discounts when purchased in bulk for premiums and sales promotions as well as for fundraising or educational use. For details, please contact us at: sales@wholechild.co

Visit us on the web at: www.wholechild.co